AMOR Y TACOS

AMOR y TACOS

MODERN MEXICAN TACOS, MARGARITAS, AND ANTOJITOS

DEBORAH SCHNEIDER
photographs by SARA REMINGTON

STEWART, TABORI & CHANG   NEW YORK

Published in 2010 by Stewart, Tabori & Chang
An imprint of Abrams

Text copyright © 2010 by Deborah Schneider
Photographs copyright © 2010 by Sara Remington
Illustrations copyright © 2010 by Nathan Pickett

Library of Congress Cataloging-in-Publication Data:
Schneider, Deborah M.
  Amor y tacos : modern Mexican tacos, margaritas, and antojitos / by Deborah Schneider.
    p. cm.
  ISBN 978-1-58479-824-8
  1. Tacos. 2. Appetizers. 3. Cocktails. 4. Cookery, Mexican. 5. Cookery--Mexico--Tijuana. I. Title.
  TX836.S36 2010
  641.5972--dc22

                    2009032240

Editor: Luisa Weiss
Designer: Alissa Faden
Production Manager: Tina Cameron

The text of this book was composed in Flama, Candida, Los Feliz, and Pacifico.

Printed and bound in China
10 9 8 7 6 5 4 3 2 1

Stewart, Tabori & Chang books are available at special discounts when purchased in quantity for premiums and promotions as well as fundraising or educational use. Special editions can also be created to specification. For details, contact specialsales@abramsbooks.com or the address below.

115 West 18th Street
New York, NY 10011
www.abramsbooks.com

ACKNOWLEDGMENTS

Writing *Amor y Tacos* was wonderful fun. How could it not be? Eating, asking dumb questions, traveling, and finally writing and testing recipes—there was no downside to this that I could see. Bows and second helpings to Luisa Weiss, my patient and talented editor, and Leslie Stoker of Stewart, Tabori & Chang, who loved the idea and were not afraid to let an author get all quirky on them. Thanks to Carole Bidnick, agent and dear, *dear* friend, for believing in me, in *Amor*, and keeping me on track. Photographer Sara Remington immersed herself with gusto in the edgier parts of Tijuana and Rosarito Beach, then had a fling in her studio with the recipes, and totally "got it," as did designer Alissa Faden. Isn't it gorgeous? ❖ Manny "It's all in the shaking" Hinojosa is a Mexico City native and a brilliantly original mixologist who created many of the recipes in the Drinks chapter and graciously gave me permission to adapt and reproduce them. Since I am a legendary lightweight in the drinking department, Manny's input was invaluable, as was the assistance and support of restaurateurs extraordinaire, Matt Baumayr and Rich Howland, my partners in SOL restaurant, as well as Jamie Waters Baumayr and Lauren "Em" Goldstein. Thank you! ❖ Being a working chef and writing is a challenging combination—even chefs have to sleep—and I couldn't do it without the best support group a chef could have, starting with my family of tasters: Barry, Willy, and Annie (who is vegan, thus proving beyond any doubt that the universe has a sense of humor.) Special thanks to dear friends and mentors David Nelson and Toni Allegra, who have been so generous with their praise and encouragement over the years. Thank you! A big *abrazo* to my family of cooks and cooking friends, past and present, who have taught me so much: in particular Manny Lopez Sr., a Tijuana native who has so generously shared his time and memories; Benito Mirafuentes, still the best cook I know; and to all my "bastard children"—you *know* who you are. Thanks for keeping me sane and making me proud. Special thanks to chef/filmmaker Joe Saldana for the golden footprint. I owe you one. ❖ Chef-owner Javier Campos of El Taco de la Ermita deserves a round of applause and a day off for so brilliantly demonstrating how truly great simple food can be. His work inspired this book. He's an original, and I am in awe. ❖ Cooking is a hard life—hard on the body, hard on the family, hard to understand sometimes why we keep doing it. And yet we do. So lastly, I want to recognize every unknown *cocinera* and great *taquero*, who live their calling every day, on the line, on the street, in hot little kitchens. Thanks for all the great food. See you soon!

CONTENTS

Introduction
9

CHAPTER 1
Cocktails, Drinks, Bebidas
18

CHAPTER 2
Antojitos
60

CHAPTER 3
Tacos
86

CHAPTER 4
Salsas and Basics
126

Sources
141

Essential Ingredients and Substitutions
143

Glossary
144

Index
150

INTRODUCTION

The idea for *Amor y Tacos* has been brewing in my notebooks for almost a decade. After publishing a book of traditional Baja Mexican recipes, and another of Mexican-inspired vegetarian food, I knew I wanted to create a "party book" of cocktails and simple, delicious food, reflecting what was happening with Mexican food on both sides of the border.

Reading back over ten years of my research journals, I found myself intrigued by the new angles on Mexican food that kept popping up in my notes, especially in the areas of tacos, antojitos (little bites), and cocktails. I started to see a new kind of Mexican food with a streetwise spin that was fun, exciting, and unexpected. I found bartenders acting like chefs; I began to see old standards done in new ways. Not fusion, but a fresh take on traditional preparations. It was food that was clearly Mexican but rethought, rediscovered, newly appreciated. I don't recall whether the light went on with my first chamoy margarita, or my first taco *vampiro*. But after my first visit to El Taco de la Ermita in Tijuana, I knew this was the direction I wanted to pursue, not least because it is rapidly becoming an even a bigger trend in the United States.

This next wave grew out of *la cocina nueva*—Mexico's answer to nouvelle cuisine and California cuisine. In every major city, especially in Mexico City, cutting-edge chefs were cooking remarkable food, and their ideas were filtering into the broader cooking community. Mexican expats who moved north to work in restaurants brought ideas with them. American chefs, finally listening to their cooks, were traveling and seeing Mexican food in a new way. Good-quality Mexican ingredients became widely available at last. Tequila suddenly became chic. It was a perfect storm.

Mexico's culinary heritage is ancient but far from static. Modern Mexican food can be stunning, precocious, ground-breaking—yet still recognizably Mexican, confidently walking the tightrope between a bone-deep understanding of tradition and the kind of head-turning, self-conscious innovation that is hip to the point of irony. You might think you know what a taco is—of course!—and yet the taco keeps evolving. A margarita is still a margarita, though flavored and tweaked in delightful new ways. Even the dreaded chips-and-salsa yawn is giving way, at last, to antojitos, wonderful little bites that showcase the cook's sophistication. The trend is definitely to simplify and emphasize freshness. Best of all, most of this food is based on the very easiest preparations: street style, quick and fast.

I wanted to present this new wave of Mexican food against the background of a real Mexican city—colorful, gritty, modern, and hip. My view of Mexico is strictly street-level. Sombreros and serapes and *molcajetes* are all very well, but these neighborhoods are alive: intriguing *botánicas*, sleekly modern Mexican design, street markets and vendors, folk art, stand-up food stalls, bubbly Mexican pop music and wailing *norteña*, wild crazy colors on walls and doors. I also wanted to share my love of funny, wry *dichos*—Mexican sayings. That's a tall order for a little book.

My first book, *¡Baja! Cooking on the Edge* introduced readers to a kind of Mexican food many didn't know existed: the food of coastal pueblos in one of the world's most beautiful and remote areas. I hope that *Amor y Tacos* will introduce you to a new kind of Mexican food and attitude and that you have as much fun exploring these new ideas as I did finding them.

AMOR ...

As a classically-trained chef who has written three books about Mexican food and the border region, I'm often asked, "Why Mexico? And for chrissakes, why *Tijuana*?" Sometimes I answer grandly, as some do about Everest, "Because it's there." (Barely 15 miles from my front door, as a matter of fact.) But the true answer is that after living in the sterile beehive of Southern California, I'm drawn to the honesty of a real city. I like the feel of being in a community where the sidewalks are crowded, you can shop and haggle, talk and laugh and stand up to eat next to strangers on the street—just like that! Like the medinas of North Africa that I visited years ago, that were the hearts of their community, Tijuana has a heart. A tough survivor's heart; a streetwise, take-no-prisoners kind of heart, but a heart you can feel, and certainly one you can come to love.

Tijuana itself is unlovely but full of life, a great, humming beast that sprawls across the dry concrete riverbed from the neatly planned streets of San Ysidro and Chula Vista. San Diego and Tijuana are like the many-headed ogre in *Monty Python and the Holy Grail*, sharing a body but occasionally fighting with itself. It's impossible for either city to escape the pulse of the other.

I've learned to appreciate the strange, funky aesthetic of this hybrid place—a noisy jigsaw of broken concrete and new high-rises, with one huarache'd foot in the past and the other on a jet ride to the future. It is alive and ever-changing, gritty, noisy, rude, colorful, and lively, full of unexpected visual gifts around every corner. A basement stairwell painted in vivid purple and yellow zebra stripes, leading nowhere. Statuettes of the busy dead, dancing, laughing, eating, and fornicating—in-your-face folk art with deadly meaning, not tourist junk. Everywhere, in odd corners, one sees loving, handmade shrines to the sweet-faced Virgin of Guadalupe, with her mantle of stars and roses, or to a local *santo* draped in rosaries and dead blossoms, dusted with the ashes of copal incense. Inside an eerie *botánica* perfumed with beeswax and incense is a semipagan mixture of herbs and potions, skeletal icons, statuettes, and good-luck charms. Outside, a string of illegible words and numbers, exquisitely rendered in spray paint, undulates down an alleyway, making a breathing dragon of a concrete wall, broken by an unused doorway framed with decades-old tiles in faded swirls and flowers.

...Y TACOS

One such neighborhood of Tijuana is home to El Taco de la Ermita (known to border cabbies, if you go, as Los Salseados), a simple open-air taqueria down a narrow street in the La Mesa area of Tijuana, just off Agua Caliente. There are hundreds of taquerias in Tijuana; you'll know you have the right place when you see a tiny place packed three deep and spilling into the road, and when you see well-dressed and wealthy *tijuanenses* (not the meekest of customers) waiting patiently for an hour or more for a precious seat. It is the only taco stand I know of that uses a uniformed security guard to keep order among its patrons.

Owner–chef auteur Javier Campos rules over a tiny outdoor kitchen built around a full-sized tree, something you can get away with only in Mexico. The best place to sit, once you elbow your way in, is the taco bar that wraps around the corner where Chef Javier works. To his left are an array of salsas in small bowls and squeeze bottles, often as many as forty different types. To his right are a small grill and a *plancha*, and one of those peculiar Mexican cooking surfaces with a concave and convex area for frying and draining *tripa* (tripe). While he cooks, he discusses the night's choices with his guests. (There is a menu, but no one orders from it.) Then, with speed and precision, he cooks, assembles tacos, dollops salsas, and peels and slices impossibly perfect avocados to place on top of each taco. He clears plates, chats amiably with everyone, barks orders at his cooks, and keeps an eye on the till and tiny table area.

The tacos are remarkable by any standard. Shrimp tacos with roasted rajas (poblanos and onions charred and sautéed with garlic and epazote) come heaped with sautéed mushrooms and no fewer than three salsas from the array at his side. Campos swiftly toasts a circle of shredded Jack cheese into a crisp golden frico (a thin disc of fried cheese), stuffs it with lobster, rolls it and tucks it into a freshly made corn tortilla with two creamy salsas, one very hot, and a sliver of perfect avocado. Slices of filet mignon are topped with garlicky shrimp and cheese and rolled up with habanero chiles and more unknown (but delicious) salsas. His tour de force is another Jack cheese frico, this one stuffed with chicken and pineapple, then topped with not one but three different fruit salsas and a sprinkle of chopped nuts. But ask for a classic, such as *tripa*, and his execution is equally flawless. The tripe is crisp and chewy, for he has been carefully cooking it for over an hour. It is served simply, with a smooth salsa verde and raw onion, and it is delicious.

El Taco is a not an isolated phenomenon, although it is better than most. Many Mexican chefs are experimenting in similar fashion. Most striking at El Taco, apart from

I found the phrase "*Amor y Tacos*" in *La Cucaracha*, a wry comic strip by Lalo Alcaraz. His recurring character, El Taco Cart Guy, is a one-man Greek chorus who comments on the world from behind his tiny cart, spatula in hand, in typically resigned fashion. One day, on the front of his cart Alcaraz scrawled the phrase *amor y tacos* as if it were the daily special. Of course! I thought, What else do you need? Shortly thereafter, I discovered the *dicho* that opens the book: *Salud, dinero y amor y tiempo para gozarlos*— "May you have health, money and love and time to enjoy them."

All that's missing is the tacos.

the sheer number of original salsas, are flavors warmly traditional, yet worlds apart from the standard taco. Campos's ingredients are often more luxurious than the average street taco—he likes filet and lobster—but he also is a master of classic salsas and ingredients like lengua (braised tongue) and tripa. His insistence on the best ingredients, perfectly fresh and chosen that day, is fanatical. Every taco is created when ordered and served with the perfect combination of salsas. And instead of handing patrons a bare taco, to be fixed *al gusto*, Javier assembles his array of salsas and creates what he thinks is the best finished product for you, a big step away from the usual taco experience. Does he know best? Absolutely. He plays those salsas like a jazz musician plays notes.

ABOUT THE *DICHOS*

When I first began working with Mexican cooks, I quickly learned that they tease each other all day long. Nicknames are casual, short, and rude: *el pelon* (baldy) for the guy who is vain about his thinning hair, *el chapparito* (shorty) for a small man in tall heels, *el gordo* (fatso) for the biggest belly or the greediest eater. I worked with several *el changitos* (apes) and one *la princesa* who happened to be male. I was called *la flaca*—the skinny one, which had other implications I won't go into here—and I was relieved to get off so lightly.

In a similar vein are the simple folk sayings known as *dichos*—often funny, sometimes bawdy, and frequently wise. There are hundreds of them, and everyone has his or her favorites. Many rhyme, the better for a semiliterate population to remember them. The first *dicho* I ever heard was along the lines of "if you're lucky in love, don't make bets"—sage advice on rolling the dice (or taking a mate for granted). When I came to work with a cold, I was advised to take a drink of mezcal or tequila because "*por todo mal, mezcal; y por todo bien, tambien*"—mezcal for all ills, and for all good, too. I learned many others: one cook, they told me, was so cheap he wouldn't buy a banana because he'd have to throw away the peel. He was so cheap he wouldn't wear glasses to read the newspaper. And so on. The cooks used to say "*poco a poco se anda lejas*"—"little by little will get you far"—which proved to be good advice for this author. I still love to hear a new *dicho*.

AMOR Y TACOS
PARTY NOTES

Tacos and antojitos are perfect party food. Almost everything can (and should) be made ahead—salsas, garnishes, tortillas—leaving just the fillings to grill or sauté at the last minute. The tacos themselves must be made by you or your guests seconds before they are eaten. *Don't* fill up a pan with premade tacos and stick it in the oven to keep warm; they'll get soggy. Instead, show off—dazzle your guests with some last-minute cooking and assemble the tacos to order, just like a *taquero*.

PLANNING This food requires more preparation time (making salsas, chopping garnishes) than assembly time. Do as much as you can in the days and hours before the party. Most salsas can be made up to 8 hours ahead; just taste them and adjust seasonings before serving. Items such as panuchos and toritos can be made a day ahead, then cooked and kept warm for up to an hour. For last-minute recipes such as ceviche and aguachiles, have all ingredients cut but separate; assemble them and then serve them right away.

- Tacos are meant to be made individually—either by the host or the guest. For a small group, the cook can assemble the tacos with just the meat. For a large group, offer everything at a buffet. Put salsas and garnishes out and allow people to finish their own tacos.

- *Dorado* and *vampiro* tacos work better for smaller groups, unless you have a large kitchen and ample assistance.

- For large groups, fish tacos are among the easiest tacos to do—just set everything out and fry or grill as you go. (I've done 600 in an hour.) Braised meats can be made the day before and reheated to serve.

- At the bar, always include a nonalcoholic beverage option.

SUGGESTED MENUS Feel free to mix and match among menus, but do avoid setting yourself up with a lot of last-minute cooking for large groups.

---

4 TO 6 GUESTS You can do almost anything for a small group, including muddling handmade margaritas.

Margarita SOL ✧ Pineapple Serrano Margarita ✧ Mexican Beer	Guacamole ✧ Salsa Quemada ✧ Tostadas ✧ Toritos	Carne Asada Tacos *Vampiros* or Shrimp Tacos *Dorados* or Mexican Hot Dogs
		Black Beans

---

8 TO 10 GUESTS Add a chilled pitcher of agua fresca as a margarita base to a self-serve bar with tequilas; add an easy-to-make substantial appetizer, served from a bowl. Once salsas and garnishes are set out, you can cook the meat and either make tacos for your guests, or allow guests make their own and add the finishing touches.

Watermelon Agua Fresca (with and without tequila) ✧ Tequilas and Sangrita ✧ Mexican Beer	Guacamole ✧ Salmon Ceviche with Ginger, Apple, and Cucumber ✧ Salsa Verde ✧ Tostadas	Chicken Fajita Tacos *Dorados* or Grilled Lamb Tacos with Salsa Borracha and Salsa Verde
		Black Beans

10 TO 15 GUESTS Set out an interactive guacamole with the drinks and add a couple of simple self-serve antojitos. Serve a big pan of carnitas that need no last-minute work, set out for everyone to make their own tacos. Rice makes the meal more substantial.

Sangria ❖ Beer ❖ La Paloma Margaritas	Rainbow Guacamole with 4 or 5 small bowls of self-serve garnishes ❖ Octopus Salpicón with Peppers, Capers, and Lemon ❖ Salsa Quemada ❖ Tostadas	Pan-Roasted Güero Chiles with Blackened Onions ❖ Lobster, Chayote, and Mango Tostadas or Salmon Ceviche with Ginger, Apple, and Cucumber ❖ Tacos of Carnitas Roasted with Orange, Milk, and Peppers
	Black Beans and Rice	

15 TO 20 GUESTS You'll need two people to assist: one to pour drinks and one to help set out the food. Offer one precooked item and one grilled or sautéed item. Let guests assemble their own tacos.

Sangria ❖ Watermelon Agua Fresca (with and without tequila) ❖ Mexican Beer	Guacamole ❖ Salmon Ceviche with Ginger, Apple, and Cucumber ❖ Salsa Quemada ❖ Salsa Verde ❖ Tostadas	Coca-Cola Shredded Beef Tacos Tacos de Lechuga with Piloncillo BBQ Shrimp (make your own) or Lemon-Garlic Chicken Tacos with Mezcal or Fish Tacos *Zarandeados*
		Black Beans and Rice

20 GUESTS AND UP Fish tacos are easy to do to order. Have all the salsas and garnishes ready, then all you have to do is fry the fish. As a second entrée have a big pan of something braised and juicy, like carnitas or shredded beef.

Sangria ❖ Watermelon and Hibiscus Aguas Frescas (with and without tequila) ❖ Bloody Marias ❖ Beer ❖ Micheladas	Tostadas ❖ Pico de Gallo ❖ Guacamole ❖ Salmon Ceviche ❖ Salsa Quemada ❖ Salsa Verde Black Beans and Rice	Deep-Fried Fish Tacos *Capeados* with Spicy Slaw or Fish Tacos *Zarandeados* Tacos of Carnitas with Orange or Coca-Cola Shredded Beef Tacos or Lengua Tacos with Tomatillo Salsa

Lo que bien se aprende, nunca se pierde.

That which is well learned is well remembered. (Practice makes perfect)

CHAPTER 1

COCKTAILS
DRINKS
BEBIDAS

Por todo mal, mezcal, y por todo bien, tambien.

For all ills, mezcal; and for all good, as well!

One should never drink without eating, and the reverse is equally true. A really good cocktail sends you off on a wet tangent, playing off the flavors of food, pairing tart and rich, sweetness and spice. Drinks are a way to enjoy pure flavor, often flavors that could not be created any other way.

If you can rethink food, why not drinks? A talented bartender brings the same creative flair to drinks as do chefs to food, utilizing fresh ingredients, stellar technique, and, often, artisanal recipes that haven't been seen for decades. Far beyond merely tending the bar (itself an honorable profession) these inspired auteurs might make their own unusual syrups and mixes from scratch, infuse alcohol with wild flavors and colors, and as a result, create drinks that are unique. Along with this comes a new respect for artisanal spirits.

Tequila is no longer just the shortest point to a party, or oblivion, but is itself worthy of serious attention. Fine estate-bottled tequilas, each painstakingly handmade, *con amor*, each one as personal as a fingerprint, are as respectable as single-malt scotches and cognacs. The cocktails in this chapter are designed to enhance tequila's herbal, earthy punch, using fresh juices and combinations that may surprise you. Every one is food-friendly, simple to make, and delicious

Note: Most of the recipes in this chapter may be made without alcohol. A thoughtful host always has a delicious nonalcoholic drink on hand for designated drivers and those who enjoy great taste for its own sake.

GIFTS OF THE AGAVE

As champagne must originate in Champagne, and cognac in Cognac, real tequila comes only from the Tequila region in Jalisco state, near the historic heart of central Mexico, where vast fields of massive blue agave plants grow in the plains and up the flanks of the mountains. When the plant is mature, which takes several years, the heart, or *piña*, is plump and full of sugars, It is then harvested and trimmed by hand, slow-roasted in a pit, or *horno* (sometimes with wood), then ground, fermented, rested, and distilled. Newly minted tequila is called *blanco* (silver) or *plata* tequila. *Reposado* has spent some time aging in oak barrels, resulting in a smoother palate and light amber color. *Añejo* may have a year or more of barrel aging, and a stiff price tag to go with its deeper color, lighter flavor, and pronounced nose. So-called super-premium tequilas may be any of these three types. They are the crème de la crème and are priced accordingly, up to hundreds of dollars a bottle. These liquid works of art should be served straight up, never mixed.

For mixed drinks, choose a moderately priced 100 percent agave tequila. Only 100 percent agave tequilas are worth your money—and if the label does not actually say 100 percent agave, it isn't. These low-agave imposters can give you a thumping headache as well.

Generally, all tequilas are better now than they were even a decade ago, thanks to a booming market fueled by sophisticated consumers and more artistic production. However, tequilas vary widely from brand to brand. Some are so smooth as to be as tasteless as vodka. At the other end of the scale, there are tequilas that have a care-fully calibrated rawness, a bigness, that thrills some people and gives others whip-lash. When you buy, don't be distracted by the lovely bottles, and don't feel as if you have to pay a lot of money. Tequila is all about taste, *your* taste—fancy packaging and high prices do not always guarantee quality.

A sipping tequila should have a clean edge, and you should be able to smell the plant, a robust, sappy, almost bitter scent. The alcohol may be mostly in the nose, or it may be a powerful part of the flavor. Texturally, tequilas range from clean and light with a slippery, silky quality, to a round, almost oily palate. Tequilas for mixed drinks should be muscular, sharp, and earthy, the better to carry the other flavors of the drink. With time, tequila becomes lighter and more subtle in flavor, losing some raw personal-ity and developing a smoother, rounder palate. Generally speaking, most *reposados* and all *añejos* will be overpowered in mixed drinks; enjoy them from a snifter. Many tequila brands now make all three, so you can taste them against each other.

Powerfully earthy mezcal (sometimes spelled mescal) is also made from agave, though distillers are not limited to the commercial blue agave. Any variety, wild or cultivated, can be used. It is made throughout Mexico, although the best estate mez-

cals come from Oaxaca. Mezcals are usually produced on small haciendas, so quality and taste can vary wildly from area to area and year to year. Mezcal is a collector's
liquor, with personality, much like single-malt scotches or great wines, and should be
enjoyed neat, with sangrita on the side. The best mezcals taste strongly of alcohol,
with a pronounced herbal/sweet/grassy "sap" flavor evocative of pepper or citrus or
even mildly bitter. Often, the primitive roasting process used imbues the mezcal with
a pleasing, subtle smokiness.

Mezcals are fascinating to drink with foods such as complex dried chile salsas, or
with sweets that temper their power and play off the smokiness.

The third gift of the agave plant is agave nectar, made from the unfermented juices of
the blue agave, boiled down to make a light syrup—the same basic idea and process
that creates maple syrup from maple sap. Unlike maple, the taste of agave nectar is
light and neutral, almost like simple syrup. It comes in light and dark versions, but
they taste virtually identical. Agave may be substituted for honey or maple syrup, or
used anywhere you would use sugar, except in baked goods.

MAKING THE PERFECT COCKTAIL

Any drink that starts with crushing ingredients in a glass (muddling) should be
made one at a time, or at most doubled to serve two. That's because a cocktail is a balance of strong spirits and flavorings, be they fruit, vegetable, syrup,
or spice. Temperature also affects flavor; so does melting ice, which slightly
smoothes and dilutes the drink. The chemistry of a drink will change if you
make bigger batches, and you will find that the drink will lose its edge, maybe
even taste a little out of whack—flat or bland.

For large groups, make a big batch of watermelon agua fresca or Bloody
Marias without the alcohol, then add the tequila as the drink is poured.

To make your task easier, work like a professional bartender. Line up your
liquors, garnishes, chilled juices, and flavorings all within reach; have rimming
salts and sugars at the ready; make sure your best stemware and glasses are
clean and polished. Then it's easy to make several drinks at a time, assembly-
line style.

OVER THE EDGE:
FINISHING THE DRINK

PRETTY LITTLE THINGS

A really beautiful drink shows attention to detail. Why just hang a lime on the glass when so many lovely garnishes can transform the cocktail into something special and echo or contrast flavor and color? As with food, the best drink garnishes are edible . . . which eliminates those little parasols. Here are some ideas.

LARGER FRUITS Choose a perfect piece of fruit that picks up on or contrasts with the color and flavor used in the cocktail. Wash it, leave the skin on, and slice it thinly or cut it into a wedge. Cut a slit in the wedge and hang it on the glass. Or add a few pieces of diced fruit to the drink. Watermelon, tangerine, starfruit, melon, apple or pear, and pineapple or mango are colorful and delicious, as are the more traditional lemon, lime, and orange.

SMALL FRUITS Drop one perfect berry or cherry into the glass, or hang it on the rim. Cut a strawberry in half, leaving the stem intact, and hang it on the glass.

CANDIED OR DRIED FRUIT Drop a couple of dried cranberries or dried mango dice into the glass, hang half a fig on the rim, or skewer the fruits on a flowering herb sprig.

HERB SPRIGS Tuck a sprig into a berry or lay a long stem of flowering herb across the top of the glass.

SHREDDED HERB Scatter finely chopped or shredded herbs on the surface of the drink.

VEGETABLES Choose fresh-looking vegetables and trim them into shapes to fit the glass and your needs. Good choices are celery hearts (white, with leaves still attached), cucumber spears, jicama sticks, avocado chunks, little tomatoes with stems, green beans, or slender asparagus spears.

CHILES Float a paper-thin slice of red Fresno or serrano chile in the drink, or split a whole small chile like a clothespin and hang it on the glass.

SEAFOOD Thread lightly cooked, chilled shrimp or scallops onto a skewer with a cherry tomato, lime, or chile on the end. Terrific with a cold beer, michelada (page 49), or vaso loco (page 50).

CHOCOLATE A little piece of bittersweet chocolate dropped into the glass, or served alongside, is especially good with mezcal or añejo tequila

RIMMING THE GLASS

Rimming the cocktail glass is a colorful detail that enhances the flavor of the cocktail. Margaritas are commonly served in a salt-rimmed glass, which makes the citrus taste sweeter and brings out the tequila flavor, but you can create many "dusts," sweet, tart, or savory.

Because you need a fine powder, it is necessary to use a mini food processor or a clean coffee-type grinder (reserve one for spices only—otherwise your coffee will flavor your spices and vice versa). Pour the finished mixture onto a small, curved dish, such as a saucer. Wipe just the edge of the glass with a wedge of lime or lemon and dip the moistened edge into the powder, to lightly coat the glass. (The dusts may also be sprinkled on the rim.) Don't overdo it—a light dusting is best. You can also dust just the inside rim of the glass; see the Margarita SOL (page 30).

Possible combinations for rimming the glasses include the following. If the mixture doesn't already come in a fine enough powder, grind it up before use.

◈ Equal parts sugar and dried orange or lemon peel

◈ Equal parts white sugar and ground dried hibiscus blossom (jamaica)

◈ Exotic sea salts—black, gray, or pink

◈ Dried chiles (guajillo, ancho, or California chiles), seeded and toasted, with a pinch of salt

◈ Lucas spice (available in Mexican markets), a combination of ground dried chiles, citrus, and salt

◈ 1 small star anise, 2 tablespoons white sugar, and a generous pinch of salt

◈ Equal parts ground Saigon cinnamon and sugar

◈ Fennel pollen (available in specialty markets) with a touch of salt

SANGRITA

Makes four 2-ounce shots. Don't confuse sangrita with the Spanish-style wine punch sangria (page 51)—it's completely different. All sangrita recipes—and there are many—include fresh citrus juice (lemon, lime, orange, or grapefruit, alone or in combination) balanced with a hint of hot sauce, salt, and acidity in the form of tomato juice or tomatillo. Think of a drinkable salsa.

- 5 ounces tomato juice
- 3 ounces fresh-squeezed lemon or lime juice, or a combination
- Pinch kosher salt, or to taste
- 1 teaspoon Mexican hot sauce such as Tapatio

Stir together all the ingredients and serve in shot glasses at room temperature with no ice.

VARIATIONS:
- ✤ Substitute orange juice for the lemon juice.
- ✤ Substitute raw tomatillos, pureed and strained, for the tomato juice.

START WITH THE SHOT: TEQUILA AND SANGRITA

Among friends in Mexico, the ceremony of tequila is handled with the greatest respect (this is *not* a spring-break-style orgy of shots, lemon, and salt). The bottle is set on the table along with small, straight-sided glasses, a bowl of limes, and little shots of sangrita—a kind of liquid palate cleanser that perfectly complements herbaceous tequila. As the hours pass, the tequila will be slowly sipped and savored, along with good food and conversation, many jokes, and little nips of the sangrita.

TEQUILA DIABLITO
(THE DEVIL'S TEQUILA)

Makes about 750 milliliters infused liquor. The name *diablito* is always a clue that there are hot chiles present—in this case, sharp little serranos whose spice is tempered with sweet mango. For a great summer variation of this spicy tequila, substitute two pints of cherry tomatoes for the mango. In winter, substitute a handful of chopped pineapple.

The recipe can be used as the basis for any infused tequila or mezcal. Use the variations suggested below or make up one of your own.

> 6 limes, well washed and thinly sliced
>
> 2 large, ripe mangoes, peeled and cubed (about 4 cups)
>
> 4 serrano chiles, split lengthwise, and seeded
>
> 1 bottle (750 ml) 100 percent agave blanco tequila

1. Pack a large glass jar or other nonreactive container with the fruit and chiles. Pour the tequila over all and infuse for 3 to 5 days, refrigerated.

2. Strain slowly through a coffee filter, without pressing down on the fruit. The infused tequila should be stored in the refrigerator and will keep for several weeks (if it lasts that long).

VARIATIONS: Use the method described for Tequila Diablito to make other kinds of infused tequila or mezcal. When you mix flavors, keep in mind that it's best to stick to one or two dominant ones.

Fruits: 4 cups fresh ripe fruit, peeled, trimmed, and thinly sliced when necessary. Try blackberry, lime, lemon, orange, tangerine, grapefruit, strawberry, mango (especially Manila mango), peach, pineapple, tamarind, melon, tart green apple, pear, pomegranate.

Vegetables: 4 cups celery, radish, cucumber, tomatillo or tomato, cut into 1-inch cubes.

Fresh Chiles: 5 or 6 chiles, stemmed and seeded. For a spicy infusion, use serranos or jalapeños (habaneros are just too hot for most people). For chile flavor without heat, use fresh Anaheims. For sweet taste and rosy color, use red bell peppers, stemmed, seeded, and cut into 1-inch pieces.

Dry Chiles: 10 guajillo (mild) or ancho (fruity), 20 chipotle (smoky and hot), or 2 cups chiles de arbol (medium-hot). Stem and seed the chiles, then dry-toast them in a hot pan and tear them into small pieces before adding the liquor.

Herbs and Flavorings: For tender, leafy fresh herbs such as cilantro, basil, mint, tarragon, lavender, use 3 cups packed, washed and patted dry. Use 2 cups packed kaffir lime leaf or thinly sliced lemongrass, and 1 to 2 cups (depending on your taste) fresh ginger, peeled and thinly sliced. Use 3 cups dry hibiscus flower (also called jamaica), crushed.

Dry Spices: Dry spices should be lightly toasted until fragrant, then roughly crushed before infusing. Use 1 cup star anise, coriander seed, cocoa nibs, allspice, or black peppercorns. Use 20 large cinnamon sticks or ¼ cup whole cloves.

TIP: If you don't want to commit a whole bottle of tequila to one flavoring, try making 1-cup batches. This will also allow you to play with various combinations. Use about a third of the ingredient amounts suggested above per cup of liquor. Infuse in a small glass jar just large enough to hold all the ingredients, so the flavorings are fully immersed in the liquor.

INFUSED TEQUILA AND MEZCAL

Tequilas are easily infused with the flavor of fruit and herbs, chiles and spices. The resulting elixirs taste terrific straight up or on ice, possibly served with a bit of infused fruit. Or you can use them in a cocktail recipe.

Mezcal's powerfully herbal, often smoky character is best enhanced with dried spices such as cinnamon, cloves, or peppercorns, and the mellow sweetness of pears or peaches, dried fruit, and honey. It is infused using the same process as for tequila.

TIP: It's best to make a strong infusion, using plenty of fruit and seasoning, so that you can have more flavor when you want it. When just a hint of flavor is what you desire, dilute the infused liquor to your taste with more tequila.

MEXICAN MOJITO

Makes 1 mojito. The mojito is so sexy and light that it would be a shame not to adapt the Cuban original to the Mexican model. Tequila is a more versatile mixer than one might think, especially in drinks that already lean to the tart and citrusy. The typical mojito is made with white rum, but a smooth white tequila works perfectly with the wisp of mint and sweetness. A very quick drink to make—and drink.

- 3 mint sprigs
- 3 lime wedges
- 3 teaspoons sugar
- 6 ounces ice cubes
- 1½ ounces 100 percent agave blanco tequila
- 2 ounces soda water or sparkling water
- 1 ounce lemon-lime soda
- Garnish: lime wheel and mint sprig

In a mixing glass or shaker, muddle the mint sprigs, lime, and sugar. Add the ice and tequila. Cap tightly, shake vigorously, and pour into a 12-ounce glass. Top up the glass with soda water and top that with the lemon-lime soda. Garnish with a sprig of mint and a lime wheel.

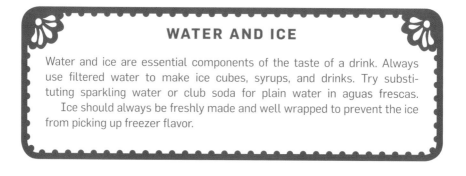

WATER AND ICE

Water and ice are essential components of the taste of a drink. Always use filtered water to make ice cubes, syrups, and drinks. Try substituting sparkling water or club soda for plain water in aguas frescas.

Ice should always be freshly made and well wrapped to prevent the ice from picking up freezer flavor.

MARGARITA SOL

Recipe makes 1 margarita, but it may be doubled to make two at a time. Merry companionship is practically guaranteed at the legendary Hussong's bar in Ensenada, especially after a couple of these tart (and very potent) margaritas. Made with fresh citrus juices and good blanco tequila, it's a simple, classic recipe that will knock you on your can if you aren't careful.

While salting the margarita rim has become commonplace, heavy salt will actually detract from the drink; try a tiny dash of salt on the ice cubes or in the bottom of the glass. I love the subtle trick of salting only the *inside* of the rim, so your lips never touch salt.

Lime wedge

Kosher salt

1½ ounces 100 percent agave blanco tequila

3 ounces fresh sweet and sour mix (recipe follows)

¾ ounce orange-flavored liqueur, such as Cointreau or Citronage

¾ ounce fresh-squeezed orange juice

Ice cubes

1. Carefully run the wedge of lime around the *inside* rim of a 12-ounce tumbler (for rocks) or a 10-ounce martini glass, then dunk the glass onto a saucer of kosher salt to create a thin line of salt around the inside rim only. Shake off excess.

2. Combine the tequila, sour mix, liqueur, and orange juice in a glass shaker filled with ice. Cap tightly, shake vigorously for 15 seconds, and strain over fresh ice cubes into the rocks glass, or straight up into the martini glass.

NOTE: Mexican bartenders make their margaritas with a distinctively flavored orange liqueur called Controy, which is unfortunately not available in this country.

FRESH SWEET AND SOUR MIX

Makes about 4 cups, enough for 8 margaritas. Sour mix is a bar staple, but most commercial bar stock is terrible stuff, full of flavorings and preservatives that shouldn't cross your lips, much less sully a good drink. This homemade mix is well-balanced between tart and sweet, but leaning toward the tart, a logical counterpoint to tequila's herbal kick. Fresh-squeezed juices are absolutely essential to the mix—don't cut corners. (Remember, *el flojo trabaja doble*—the lazy person works twice as hard.) The work of juicing is a small price to pay for the most delicious drinks ever!

TIP: Room-temperature fruit yields more juice.

    1 cup fresh-squeezed lemon juice
    1 cup fresh-squeezed lime juice
    ⅓ cup white sugar
    2 cups filtered water

Combine all the ingredients and refrigerate. Depending on the sweetness of the fruit, you may want to add a little more sugar or water, but keep a nice tart edge. Use within 24 hours.

MODERN MARGARITA

Makes 1 margarita. This cocktail has all the citrus flavor you expect from a margarita, but you don't have to juice the fruit first. Agave nectar, tapped from the same blue agave from whose hearts tequila is distilled, adds a gentle sweetness that softens the taste of citrus and bold tequila. Because the drink is made with muddled fruit, it will have a slight, pleasant bitterness from the peel.

2 lemon slices

2 lime slices

2 orange slices

Ice cubes

1½ ounces 100 percent agave blanco
   tequila

¾ ounce orange-flavored liqueur,
   such as Cointreau or Citronage

¾ ounce agave nectar (simple syrup
   may be substituted, see page 37)

In a mixing glass or shaker, muddle the citrus slices. Add ice, tequila, liqueur, and agave nectar, cap tightly, and shake vigorously for 15 seconds. Strain into a chilled 10-ounce martini glass or over fresh ice cubes into a 12-ounce tumbler.

LIMONADA

Makes 1 drink. This is a big *turista* mouthful. You'll find it (along with many variations) in the resort bars along the Mexican coast. Some enterprising vacationer must have thought that if lime in beer was tasty, adding a whole margarita to a beer must be better still, and the combination of bitterness, lime, and bubbles is unabashedly refreshing. The drink is basically a strong, effervescent margarita, served in a large goblet (schooner) with a beer, bottle and all, upside down in it. Lift the beer up so it pours out to fill the glass. Drink ice-cold.

  Ice cubes

2 ounces 100 percent agave blanco
  tequila

1 ounce simple syrup (page 37) or
  light agave nectar

1 ounce soda water or sparkling
  water

1 ounce grapefruit soda such as
  Squirt or Fresca

1 ounce lime juice

1 Mexican beer, such as Pacifico or
  Bohemia, very cold

In a shaker filled with ice, combine the tequila, syrup, soda water, grapefruit soda, and lime juice. Shake until well chilled and strain into a 16-ounce beer goblet. Pop the top on the beer and quickly turn it upside down in the glass, so the beer stays in the bottle. Serve right away with the bottle still in the glass.

TANGERINE GINGER MARGARITA

Makes 1 margarita. If you remember when the Tequila Sunrise ruled bar menus across the land, you will recognize the roots of this elegant drink—but any similarity stops there. The lovely pale-pink color comes from pomegranate juice, and the drink has just the slightest hint of ginger.

- 4 slices peeled fresh ginger
- 2 slices tangerine or orange
- Ice cubes
- 1½ ounces 100 percent agave blanco tequila
- 1 ounce simple syrup (page 37)
- 1 ounce fresh-squeezed lime juice
- 2 ounces pomegranate juice
- Garnish: pomegranate seeds or thin slice of ginger, unpeeled

In a shaker, crush the ginger and tangerine slices. Top with ice, tequila, syrup, lime juice, and pomegranate juice. Cover tightly and shake for 15 seconds, until well chilled. Strain into a martini glass and garnish with a few pomegranate seeds or cut a slit in the ginger slice and slip it onto the rim.

PINEAPPLE SERRANO MARGARITA

Makes 1 margarita. A terrific and unique margarita, sweet and spicy with fragrant pineapple and fiery serrano chiles. Don't strain this one—pour the crushed fruit and chiles over the ice allowing the flavors to continue to meld. The drink will get spicier toward the end, as the heat from the serrano escalates, but it will be balanced by the bits of pineapple. You'll eat every bit.

- 3 chunks ripe, fresh pineapple or canned in juice
- 2 slices serrano chile
- Ice cubes
- 1½ ounces 100 percent agave blanco tequila
- 1 ounce fresh-squeezed lime juice
- 2 ounces simple syrup (page 37)
- **Garnish:** unpeeled pineapple wedge

In a 10-ounce rocks glass, crush the pineapple and chiles together with a muddler. Fill the glass with ice and pour in the tequila, lime juice, and syrup. Stir with a long-handled spoon. Cut a slit in the pineapple wedge and slide it onto the rim of the glass.

FLAVORING SYRUPS, AGAVE, OR HONEY

Simple syrup is a bartender's secret ally, a hint of sweetness that unites and balances the disparate flavors in a cocktail. If you prefer, honey or agave may be used in place of a sugar syrup.

Syrups may be enhanced with many of the same flavors used to infuse tequila (page 26), often with stunning results. I love a syrup made with hot chiles! These infused syrups are terrific in nonalcoholic beverages such as iced tea or juice drinks as well. Syrups, whether flavored or not, and infused honey or agave should always be stored in the refrigerator, covered, where they will keep indefinitely.

SIMPLE SYRUP

Makes about 2 cups.

2 cups water

2 cups granulated cane sugar, preferably superfine or bartender's sugar

Whisk sugar and water together in a small, heavy pan. Bring to a boil, reduce the heat, and simmer for about 5 minutes, whisking occasionally, until the sugar is completely dissolved.

NOTE: Regular granulated sugar may be substituted for the superfine. It will just take a little longer to dissolve completely.

VARIATIONS:

❖ For flavored syrup, simmer your choice of flavoring from the list below with the sugar water for 30 minutes, over gentle heat. Remove from heat and cool. Leave the flavoring in the syrup for 24 hours before straining.

❖ To infuse fresh herbs such as mint, thyme, or rosemary, pour the boiling syrup over a ½ cup herbs and immediately remove from heat. Let sit for 4 hours, then strain.

❖ To infuse agave nectar or honey, be sure to use a pasteurized product. Gently warm the syrup with the chosen flavorings over low heat, then steep 48 hours in the refrigerator before straining.

- Zest of 2 washed lemons, oranges, limes, tangerines, or grapefruits
- ½ cup of any of the herbs, fruit, or spices from the infused tequila list (page 26)
- ½ cup ground espresso coffee beans
- 1 cup peeled, chopped fresh ginger or lemongrass
- 4 vanilla beans, split lengthwise
- 2 dried ancho or guajillo chiles, toasted, stemmed, seeded, and torn into small pieces

WATERMELON AGUA FRESCA

Makes about 5 cups. Fresh juices are not optional; they're essential. Most concentrates taste both fake and foul and store-bought juices are often loaded with corn syrup, artificial colors, and flavors. A lever-type hand juicer or juice appliance makes the task of juicing fresh fruit easy, and the flavor is incomparable.

Aguas frescas are healthy, flavorful fruit drinks popular in Mexico. They are simply made: mashed fresh fruit and water flavored with a touch of lime juice and perhaps a little agave nectar or sugar. Think lemonade, only not as sweet, and made from almost any kind of fruit. To turn any agua fresca into a cocktail, just add tequila or rum. The following recipe is a good basic recipe.

2 cups cubed seedless watermelon
or other very ripe fruit

3 cups water

Fresh-squeezed juice of 1 lime

1 tablespoon agave nectar or cane
sugar (if desired)

Garnish: lime wedge

Mash the fruit to a pulp. Stir in the water, lime juice, and sweetener. Chill well. Serve over ice with a lime wedge.

VARIATIONS:
- ❖ Cucumber and melon
- ❖ Fennel and apple
- ❖ Tamarind
- ❖ Lemons and limes
- ❖ Mango
- ❖ Guava
- ❖ Papaya
- ❖ Pineapple
- ❖ Jamaica (hibiscus flower)

SPICY VERDE
(GREEN MARIA)

Makes 1 drink. Not everyone is a fan of sweet, fruity drinks. Tequila's crisp, edgy flavor is just as delicious in this vegetable-spiked cocktail. For a drink so simple, the flavors are vibrant and clean. The celery and spiciness are reminiscent of a Bloody Maria, but without the tomato. Perhaps it is an invisible Maria?

NOTE: The closer you cut to the stem end of the jalapeño, the spicier the slice of pepper will be.

½ celery stick, split and cut into
 ½-inch pieces

6 sprigs cilantro

1 thin slice jalapeño

Ice cubes

1½ ounces 100 percent agave blanco
 tequila

½ ounce fresh-squeezed lime juice

Garnish: celery stick with leaves

In a 10-ounce rocks glass, crush the celery, cilantro, and jalapeño with a muddler. Fill the glass with ice and pour in the tequila and lime juice. Stir well and serve with a stick of celery, preferably with leaves.

BLACKBERRY MINT MARGARITA

Makes 1 drink. Sweet without being cloying, this refreshing drink is a classic example of the "new" seasonal cocktail, based on fresh herbs and fruit. Make it when summer berries are ripe and bursting with flavor and rich color. It can be adapted with tarragon, lemon balm, or other herbs in place of, or along with, the mint.

4 large, juicy blackberries

8 fresh mint leaves

Ice cubes

$\frac{1}{2}$ ounce agave nectar

2 ounces 100 percent agave blanco
  tequila

1 ounce fresh-squeezed lime juice

1 ounce sparkling wine

Garnish: blackberry decorated with a
  mint sprig or a mint leaf

In a shaker, use a muddler to crush the mint leaves, then the blackberries. Fill with ice and add the agave, tequila, and lime juice. Cover tightly and shake vigorously for 30 seconds. Strain into a chilled martini glass and top up with a splash of chilled sparkling wine. Perch a blackberry on the rim and tuck a mint sprig into it like a stem, or just float a mint leaf in the drink.

HIBISCUS MARGARITA

Makes 1 drink. This is a perfectly beautiful drink, made with or without alcohol. Mexican aguas frescas are drinks made of fresh fruit and water, sweetened and sparked with a squeeze of fresh lime—the perfect drink on a hot day, and healthy as well. Dried hibiscus flowers (*jamaica* in Spanish) make a hot-pink agua fresca with an excitingly tart, fruity flavor. Dried jamaica is sold in bulk at Mexican markets.

- 1 tablespoon white sugar
- 1 teaspoon ground cinnamon
- Lime wedge
- Ice cubes
- 4 ounces hibiscus syrup (recipe follows)
- 1½ ounces 100 percent agave blanco tequila
- 1 ounce sparkling water
- Garnish: lime wedge or cinnamon stick

1. Combine the sugar and cinnamon on a small plate. Moisten the rim of the glass with the lime wedge, dip the glass in the cinnamon sugar, and shake off the excess.

2. Fill a 12-ounce glass with ice and pour in the tequila and hibiscus syrup. Top up with sparkling water. Stir carefully. Squeeze the juice from the lime wedge you used to prepare the glass rim on top of the drink and discard the wedge. Garnish with a fresh wedge of lime or a cinnamon stick.

VARIATION: Chill a 7-ounce martini glass and prepare the rim as described. In a shaker jar, combine the ice, hibiscus syrup and tequila, along with 1 tablespoon Cointreau or Grand Marnier. Cover tightly, shake well for 15 seconds, and strain into the glass. Garnish with a thin slice of lime.

HIBISCUS SYRUP

Makes about 3½ cups. Use this syrup as a base for drinks or freeze it into a delicious sorbet.

    4 cups water
    2 cups white sugar
    2 cups dried hibiscus flower (jamaica)

1. Combine all ingredients in a saucepan and simmer over low heat until the sugar is dissolved, stirring often. Cook at a slow simmer for 30 minutes.

2. Let stand for 2 hours (or as long as overnight), then strain into a storage jar, pressing down on the flowers. Keeps indefinitely refrigerated.

BAR EQUIPMENT

A few simple gadgets will make not only make bartending easier and more fun, but will also produce professional-looking results.

- A collection of various kinds of glasses (martini glass, 12-ounce rocks glass, 14-ounce tall glass, wineglass, shot glass, snifter)

- Ounce measure (jigger) with demarcations of ½ ounce, ¾ ounce, 1 ounce, and 1½ ounces

- Handheld citrus juicer—the type with a hinge—or a wooden reamer and a small sieve to catch the seeds

- Blender

- Long, slender metal spoon for stirring

- 1-quart measuring cup

- Pint glass for mixing and muddling

- Metal cocktail shaker with tight-fitting lid

- Bartender's strainer

- Muddling stick (looks like a miniature baseball bat) for crushing fruit and herbs

SEXY MARGARITA
(OR MARGARITA AMOR)

Makes 1 margarita. Admit it, the name caught your eye, didn't it? Damiana is a liqueur brewed in Mexico from a wild herb (*Turnera diffusa* or *Turnera aphrodisiaca*) that has been used as an aphrodisiac and gentle mood-elevator since prehistoric times. The bottle is shaped like a robust naked woman, and—ironically, perhaps—the liqueur tastes rather like that monkish treat, Benedictine.

- 2 lemon slices
- 2 lime slices
- 2 orange slices
- Ice cubes
- 1½ ounces 100 percent agave blanco tequila
- ½ ounce Damiana
- ¾ ounce agave nectar
- 1 lime wedge

In a mixing glass or shaker, muddle the lemon, lime, and orange slices. Add ice, tequila, Damiana, and agave nectar and shake vigorously for 15 seconds. Strain into a chilled 10-ounce martini glass or pour over fresh ice cubes into a 12-ounce tumbler. Squeeze the lime wedge on top and discard.

WATERMELON MARGARITA
WITH CANDIED CACTUS

Makes 1 margarita. Watermelon (*sandia*) is one of Mexico's best-loved fruits, often served with a squeeze of lime and a sprinkle of chile powder to bring out the juicy sweetness, or crushed with water and lime to make a favorite agua fresca. This drink playfully echoes those tastes, with a hint of mild guajillo chiles, basil to cut the sweetness and enhance the tequila flavors, and, just for fun, a sliver of candied cactus as a garnish. Look for candied cactus, or *viznaga*, at well-stocked Mexican markets. If you can't find it, substitute candied watermelon rind or a triangular sliver of fresh watermelon with the green rind left on.

1 lime
Ground California or guajillo chiles
1 cup seedless watermelon cubes
2 fresh basil leaves
1 teaspoon agave nectar
Ice cubes
1½ ounces 100 percent agave blanco
    tequila
Garnish: candied cactus

1. Chill a large martini glass. Juice the lime and reserve the juice. Rub the rim of the glass with a piece of the lime rind and dust with a delicate layer of chile.

2. In a shaker, crush the watermelon and basil together. Add the lime juice, agave nectar, ice, and tequila. Cover tightly and shake vigorously for 15 seconds. Strain into the rimmed glass and garnish with a thin slice of candied cactus.

LA PALOMA MARGARITA

Makes 1 margarita. No one knows why this popular drink is called *la paloma*—the dove. It may have been in homage to a lovely woman. Or perhaps it is the pale color and smoothness of this easy-drinking combination that inspired the name. Don't be fooled, though—this drink is seductively potent. Overindulge one evening and the next morning you may find yourself broke and alone, wondering who she was. Use an excellent tequila with a sharp, edgy character. The pinch of salt gives the cocktail perfect balance.

Ice cubes

Pinch of kosher salt

2 ounces 100 percent agave blanco tequila

½ ounce fresh-squeezed lime juice

Mexican Squirt (or grapefruit soda such as Fresca), chilled

Garnish: lime wheel

Fill a 12-ounce tumbler with ice. Sprinkle the salt over the ice and add the tequila and lime juice. Top up with the grapefruit soda, and garnish with a lime wheel.

RICO SUAVE

Makes 1 drink. Tequila, always surprisingly versatile, makes an excellent diges-tif. Añejo tequilas rest in barrels for up to a year before bottling, which softens the brashness of the nose and flavor profile. This rich, smooth drink fuses the mellow-ness of the tequila with a touch of complex, honeyed Cointreau Noir (a blend of Coin-treau and cognac) and the tiniest spritz of bitter orange oil. Serve the cocktail in a snifter, and consider pairing it with squares of excellent varietal chocolates rich in cocoa butter and with a hint of bitterness, such as those created by Valrhona or Scharffen Berger. This is love in a glass.

½ ounce Cointreau Noir

1½ ounces best-quality 100 percent
agave añejo tequila

2-inch strip orange peel

Combine the Cointreau Noir and tequila in a snifter. Twist the orange peel over the drink to release the oils into it. You may drop the peel into the glass or serve without.

Mira a tu suegra como
a las estrellas... de lejos...

Look at your mother in law as if
she was a star... from far away.

MICHELADA

Makes 1 drink. On a hot day, the michelada is the most refreshing drink ever, though the combination of bitter beer, Clamato, spice, chiles, and lime might strike some as bizarre. To me it is the essence of Mexico: a searing beach, a shady *palapa*, and an ice-cold michelada in hand, giving one the strength to get through the afternoon. There are, of course, as many michelada variations as there are bartenders—and that's before they start filling your glass with plump shrimp, encouraging you to down the drink even faster. (This is called a *perfecta*, and if the idea appeals to you, check out the *vaso loco* on the next page.) Be sure to freeze the glass for the full effect.

Lucas spice* or dry pico de gallo
  spice
2 ounces Clamato juice
5 dashes of Maggi seasoning
5 dashes of Mexican hot sauce such
  as Cholula
2 limes
Ice-cold Mexican beer

Place a 12-ounce tumbler in the freezer for about 30 minutes. Rub the rim of the tumbler with a cut lime, and dip it in the Lucas spice. Add the Clamato and seasonings. Squeeze the limes directly into the glass. Top up with the beer.

VARIATIONS:

❖ Omit the Clamato and seasonings and add the juice of 1 more lime.

❖ Perfecta—add several plump, cooked shrimp to the glass. Drink the beer, eat the shrimp.

❖ Beer Diablito—substitute sangrita (page 24) for the Clamato, add a dash of hot sauce.

❖ Beer Limonada—salt the rim of the glass; mix beer with an equal amount of Fresca or Squirt; top with a squeeze of lime.

*Ground spice mixes made with chiles and salt, available at Mexican markets; pico de gallo is spicy, the other mild.

VASO LOCO
(WILD THING)

Makes 1 drink. The *vaso loco* (literally, "crazy glass") is an elaborate version of the *michelada* (previous page). Filled with seafood, it is as much a snack as a drink. It's always great fun to see what an inventive *cantinero* puts together. The basic elements are fresh shellfish (usually cooked, but not always), something tomatoey, beer, citrus, spices, and a shot of tequila floating on top.

Lightly cooked shrimp, clams, scallops, singly or in combination, to half-fill glass

Clam juice as needed

Chilled Clamato juice, sangrita (page 24), or tomato juice

Ice-cold Mexican beer, as needed

$\frac{1}{2}$ ounce blanco tequila

Half a lime

Garnish: Cucumber stick or jicama stick

For serving: store-bought or homemade hot sauce (page 131), lime wedges

Prepare a 12-ounce glass as for michelada (page 49). Fill the glass half full of seafood and add enough clam juice to barely cover the seafood. Add 1 inch of Clamato, sangrita, or juice. Fill the glass with beer and serve the rest of the beer on the side. Carefully float the tequila on top of the drink and squeeze the lime over all; do not stir. Garnish with a cucumber or jicama stick. Serve with a spoon, hot sauce, and more limes.

VARIATIONS:

❖ Garnish the drink with more seafood—for example, a chipotle-spiced grilled shrimp on a skewer along with a cherry pepper and a cherry tomato. Or skewer a shrimp and a whole serrano chile on a rosemary sprig.

❖ Half fill the glass with small pieces of raw shrimp and scallop. Cover with fresh lime juice, add a finely minced serrano chile, stir, and wait 5 minutes. Continue with the Clamato, beer, and tequila.

SANGRIA

This makes 6 to 8 servings. When it's hot, nothing tastes better than chilled sangria, which is as popular in Mexico as in its native Spain. Mexicans often make sangria with one of the powerful, heat-concentrated red wines that have been made in Baja California since the eighteenth century.

1 lime

1 lemon

1 orange

1 bottle inexpensive red wine, such as syrah or zinfandel

½ cup brandy or white rum

2 pieces star anise

1 cinnamon stick

Sliced seasonal fruit (grapes, peaches, apples, pears, and melon are traditional, but mango, pineapple, or berries also work well)

Ice cubes

Sparkling water, soda water, or sparkling wine

Garnish: sliced fruit

1. Wash the citrus fruits, cut them in half, and slice them into ¼-inch-thick slices. Place them in a large glass pitcher and add the wine, brandy, and spices. Cover and steep overnight in the refrigerator.

2. To serve, put some fresh fruit in the bottom of a wine glass or tall glass. Fill three-quarters full with ice cubes. Strain the sangria into the glass until the ice is just covered. Top off the glass to the rim with sparkling water or wine. Cut a slit in a piece of fruit and hang it on the rim.

NOTE: For a faster sangria, mash the lemons, limes, and oranges in the pitcher with the spices and pour the wine over. Let stand 30 minutes, strain, and proceed with the recipe.

VARIATION: To make a hibiscus sangria, slice up an orange, a lime, a lemon, and a green apple, and place them in a large glass pitcher. Half fill the pitcher with hibiscus syrup (page 44) and refrigerate for several hours or overnight. Top up with sparkling wine (or, for a nonalcoholic version, sparkling water) and pour into ice-filled glasses. Garnish with more fresh fruit.

VAMPIRA

Serves 1. The *vampira* is tall, spicy, tart, and refreshing. It's essentially a revved-up version of the margarita with the barest touch of Clamato and spicy edge, and just as brunch-friendly as the Bloody Maria. This excellent version of the cocktail is served at Restaurante Romesco in San Diego, where it is made with a high-end tequila and a dash of Clamato.

Ice cubes

Pinch of salt

1½ ounces 100 percent agave blanco
   tequila

1 teaspoon Mexican hot sauce such
   as Cholula

1 ounce Clamato juice

1 ounce fresh-squeezed lemon juice

Mexican Squirt or other grapefruit
   soda

Garnish: lemon wedge

Fill a 10-ounce glass with ice cubes. Scatter salt on the ice. Pour in the tequila, hot sauce, Clamato, and lemon juice, and top up the glass with the grapefruit soda. Garnish with a lemon wedge.

BLOODY MARIA

Makes 1 drink. In spite of some mumblings about Hemingway and Cuba being the source of the Bloody Mary, many sources agree that the drink is suspiciously similar to sangrita (page 24), a spicy, tomato-based concoction that is traditionally served alongside straight tequila shots. If you're a Mary drinker, you'll like this tequila variation.

Lime wedge

Lucas spice* or dry pico de gallo
 spice

Ice cubes

4 ounces sangrita (page 24)

1½ ounces 100 percent agave blanco
 tequila

Garnish: jicama or cucumber stick

Run the lime around the rim of a 12-ounce glass and dip the glass into the spice. Fill with ice cubes. Pour sangrita over the ice and pour the tequila on top. Garnish with a stick of jicama or cucumber.

*Ground spice mixes made with chiles and salt, available at Mexican markets; pico de gallo is spicy, the other mild.

MORDIDA DEL CHUPACABRA
(BITE OF THE CHUPACABRA)

Makes 1 drink. Mexico has a Sasquatch of its own: the legendary *chupacabra* (literally, "goat sucker"), a squat, hairy . . . um . . . *thing*, which sucks the blood out of small animals in the night and can presumably be conjured up by Mami to keep naughty children in line. Most of your encounters with chupacabras will be in daylight at the local juice stand, where the popular mixture of fresh fruit, beet, and other vegetable juices makes a healthy (if blood-colored) start to the day. The juice forms the base for an excellent, unusual, and very healthy cocktail.

1½ ounces 100 percent agave blanco
    tequila

8 ounces chupacabra juice (recipe
    follows)

Garnish: lemon wedge and skewered
    fresh vegetable chunks (such as
    cherry tomato, cucumber, olive,
    jicama, celery) or a celery stalk

Fill a 14-ounce glass with ice cubes, then pour in the tequila and chupacabra juice. Garnish with a lemon wedge and skewered vegetables or a celery stalk.

VARIATIONS:

✤ Rim the glass with ground chile powder or black sea salt (see page 53 for technique).

✤ Crush a slice of jalapeño in the bottom of the glass before adding ice, or add a dash or two of bottled hot sauce.

JUGO DE CHUPACABRA

Makes 3 cups. Adjust the proportions of the juices to suit your taste, if desired.

- 8 ounces fresh-squeezed orange juice
- 4 ounces fresh carrot juice
- 2 ounces fresh celery juice
- 4 ounces fresh pineapple juice
- 8 ounces fresh beet juice

Stir all ingredients together in a pitcher or storage jar.

VARIATIONS:
- ✤ Substitute tomato juice for beet juice.
- ✤ Substitute pomegranate juice for beet juice.
- ✤ Substitute more pineapple juice for half the orange juice.

Si barbas valieran, todos los chivos jefes fueran.

If a beard made you smart, then goats would rule us.

ICED MEXICAN COFFEE

Makes 1 drink. Café de olla is a sweet, heavily spiced brew, usually taken hot in the morning with sweet rolls and in the afternoon with crunchy cookies or a pastry. This refreshing dessert drink, served over ice, features café de olla's welcome kick of caffeine.

1 tablespoon chocolate syrup in a squeeze bottle

Ice cubes

4 ounces café de olla (recipe follows), chilled

2 ounces liquor such as coffee liqueur, brandy, dark rum or almond-flavored liqueur

1 tablespoon heavy cream, condensed milk, or whipped cream

Small pinch of ground cinnamon

Chill a 12-ounce glass. Drizzle the inside of the glass with the chocolate syrup, then fill the glass with ice and pour in the liquor. Top up with chilled café de olla. Drizzle the cream on top (or spoon on the whipped cream) and dust with cinnamon.

CAFÉ DE OLLA

Makes 4 cups. Café de olla is also great as a float, topped with a scoop of vanilla ice cream. Piloncillo is raw cane sugar, molded and sold in cones. It has a mild molasses flavor; raw sugar or brown sugar may be substituted.

5 cups water

4 large cinnamon sticks

6 whole cloves

4 star anise

1 cone piloncillo sugar (or ½ cup firmly packed brown sugar)

¾ cup ground espresso coffee beans, regular or decaffeinated

Combine the water, spices, and sugar in a small saucepan. Bring slowly to a boil over medium heat, stirring occasionally to break up the sugar. Reduce the heat and simmer gently, without stirring, for 30 minutes. Remove from the heat, stir in the coffee, cover, and steep for 5 minutes. Line a sieve with a coffee filter and strain the coffee through it. Serve hot or, for iced coffee, store in the refrigerator, covered, for up to 1 week.

HOT CHOCOLATE
WITH AGAVE AND ALMONDS

Makes 1 cup. Definitely rich, and delicious enough for dessert. Chocolate is native to Mexico, where it is whipped into a light-flavored, frothy drink, fragrant with soft Mexican cinnamon and slightly gritty with sugar and almonds. Here, the flavors are enhanced with crema de almendrado, an almond-flavored liqueur based on agave nectar. If you can't find it, any almond liqueur (such as Amaretto) may be substituted.

- 6 ounces milk
- 1 ounce Ibarra-brand Mexican chocolate, about ¼ disk
- 1½ ounces crema de almendrado (or other almond liqueur)
- Whipped cream
- Freshly grated nutmeg

1. Heat the milk with the chocolate, stirring often with a whisk. Do not allow the mixture to boil. Add the crema de almendrada and heat through. Using a wire whisk, whip until frothy and light.

2. Pour into a heated mug and top with a dollop of whipped cream, then grate a tiny wisp of nutmeg onto the cream. Serve hot.

VARIATION: Substitute 1 tablespoon raspberry-flavored liqueur and 1 tablespoon brandy for the crema de almendrada. Substitute a drizzle of chocolate syrup for the nutmeg.

CHAPTER 2

ANTOJITOS

Tierra que fueres, haz lo que vieres.

Wherever you go, behave as they do.

Antojitos are Mexico's small-plate offerings, falling in size somewhere between a meal and a snack—similar to tapas or mezes. The antojito is an impulsive indulgence, the kind of savory goodie you just can't pass up. Not something you need, but certainly something you really *want*, to accompany drinks and conversation with friends, or to deliciously fill the gaps between lunch, the evening meal, and a late (in Mexico, often very late) bedtime. Antojitos should be fun—light and frivolous, even amusing. The best of them pack a world of flavor into just a few bites. And they make terrific party food.

By definition, antojitos are easy to make and readily adaptable to what you have on hand. Perfect examples are the guacamoles, with their countless combinations, and the panucho, a corn masa empanada which can be stuffed with almost anything and tarted up with an infinity of salsas and garnishes. Of course the *perro caliente*, the Mexican hot dog (page 80), is in a class by itself, as is a ceviche made with raw beef.

Here is the cook's chance to dazzle. This is no time for subtlety, but an opportunity to engage all the senses and have fun with flavor, heat, color, texture. Many of the recipes in this chapter will become jumping-off points for your own taste and inspirations, defined by the season and your guests.

TORITOS

(LITTLE PEPPERS STUFFED WITH GARLIC, SHRIMP, AND OAXACA CHEESE)

Makes 8 stuffed peppers. Test the collective machismo of your gathering with these delicious little peppers oozing with cheese, garlic, and sweet shrimp. I like to use different colors of small peppers—an ensemble of yellow güero, jalapeño, and red "lipstick" or other sweet miniature peppers looks particularly attractive. If you use jalapeños or güeros, they will definitely be spicy. Toritos take just a minute to make, and they can be prepared ahead and finished in the oven. The fillings can be varied according to the season; sautéed sweet corn is a very good addition.

8 small pointed peppers, about 3 inches long, such as jalapeño, güero, miniature sweet peppers, or lipstick (red Fresno) peppers

1 tablespoon butter

1½ teaspoons minced fresh garlic

1 green onion, trimmed and thinly sliced

4 ounces (about 10) medium raw shrimp, peeled, deveined, and coarsely chopped to yield about ¾ cup

¼ teaspoon salt

¾ cup shredded good-quality Oaxaca, Jack, or mozzarella cheese

To serve: mango habanero salsa (page 136), pomegranate seeds or toasted pepitas (optional), cilantro sprigs

1. Wash and dry the chile pepper, leaving the stems on. Wearing disposable gloves to keep the hot oil off your skin, cut a slit down one side of each pepper. Use a slim, blunt knife or a tool such as the handle of a teaspoon to carefully scrape out all the seeds. Work carefully so you don't break the pepper or dislodge its stem.

2. In a 10-inch sauté pan, melt the butter over medium-low heat. Add the garlic and green onion and cook until fragrant, but not browned. Add the chopped shrimp, season with salt, and cook, stirring often, until the shrimp are pink and firm. Remove from heat and cool to room temperature, about 10 minutes.

3. Stir in the shredded cheese. The mixture should hold its shape. If it is too crumbly, turn it out on a cutting board and chop until it sticks together.

4. Use a small teaspoon to gently fill each pepper with about 1½ tablespoons of the

shrimp mixture. The filling should be generous. At this point, if you wish, you can refrigerate the stuffed peppers, covered, for up to 24 hours.

5. Preheat the oven to 350 degrees. Heat an ovenproof cast-iron griddle or pan over medium-high heat. Lay a sheet of foil on the griddle and set the peppers on top. Roast the peppers on all sides until they are browned in places and are starting to get soft and wrinkled.

6. Transfer the griddle or pan to the oven and bake for 5 to 7 minutes, until the filling is hot and bubbly.

7. Arrange the stuffed peppers on a warm serving plate and top each with a spoonful of mango salsa. Scatter with the pomegranate seeds or pepitas, if using, and serve right away with cilantro sprigs.

VARIATIONS:

- ❖ Fill with roughly mashed black beans (page 140) and a sprinkle of cotixa cheese (serve with pico de gallo, page 128, or tomatillo salsa).

- ❖ Fill with queso fresco and chopped fresh epazote (serve with pico de gallo).

- ❖ Turn the stuffed chile inside out—roast the chiles unstuffed, then fill them with mango salsa and top each with a whole shrimp sautéed in butter and garlic.

PANUCHOS
CON QUESO Y FLOR DE CALABASA
(CORN EMPANADAS WITH CHEESE AND ZUCCHINI FLOWERS)

Makes 12 panuchos. Half-moon-shaped panuchos are a variation on a Yucatecan recipe made from fresh corn masa dough, stuffed with a delicious filling of gooey cheese and delicate zucchini flowers, fried until crisp, and served topped with black beans, crema, and salsa. (In the Yucatán, the beans are frequently on the inside.) The filling used here is typically Mexican, but you might come up with your own, less traditional variations. Lard is often used for frying panuchos, but vegetable oil or shortening or a combination, may be substituted here. For a leaner version, cook them on a lightly oiled griddle; they will become more like traditional quesadillas.

Spicy masa (recipe follows)

4 ounces crumbled cotixa cheese (divided use)

16 large zucchini flowers (see note)

5 ounces shredded Oaxaca or Jack cheese

¼ cup epazote leaves, finely shredded

4 green onions, sliced

Fresh lard*, vegetable shortening, or oil, for frying

Black beans (page 140)

½ cup crema fresca or sour cream

Pico de gallo (page 128)

Sliced pickled jalapeños

1 cup shredded iceberg lettuce (optional)

1. Form the masa into 12 equal pieces, each about the size of a golf ball, cover, and set aside. Measure out ¼ cup of the cotixa cheese and set it aside for finishing the dish.

2. Rinse the zucchini flowers quickly in a bowl of cold water, drain, and pat dry with a clean towel. Roughly chop the flowers into ½-inch pieces.

3. Mix the remaining cotixa cheese, the Oaxaca cheese, epazote, and green onions. Toss the mixture with the zucchini blossoms.

4. Line a tortilla press with plastic squares (squares cut from clean, unused plastic grocery bags work well). Gently press out a masa ball to about 3½ inches in diameter. Leave the masa on the plastic. Place a heaping tablespoon of filling on one side of the masa circle. Use the plastic to fold the masa circle in half, and gently press down all over the panucho, lightly compressing the cheese and completely sealing edges

*Fresh lard is sometimes available at Mexican supermarkets with delis, where it is a by-product of carnitas. It is semi-liquid and has a wonderful "roast pork" flavor. White lard may be substituted.

around it. Peel off the plastic and set the panucho on a cookie sheet; cover with a dry kitchen towel.

5. Repeat the proecess with the remaining masa. If the masa begins to crack, dip two fingers into water and work the moisture well into the dough ball before pressing. At this point, the panuchos may be wrapped and refrigerated for up to 24 hours.

6. In a 10-inch sauté pan over medium heat, melt enough lard to have it a ½-inch deep. Fry the panuchos in the lard on both sides until golden brown and crisp, about 2 minutes per side. Drain briefly on paper towels.

7. Serve the panuchos hot, topped with a spoonful of beans, a dab of cream, a generous spoonful of pico de gallo, the reserved cotixa cheese, the jalapeños, and the shredded lettuce on top for crunch, if you like.

NOTE: Zucchini flowers are in season for a short time in the summer. If they are not available, shredded fresh spinach or minced raw zucchini may be substituted.

VARIATIONS:
  ✦ Add chopped cooked chorizo or shrimp in step 3.
  ✦ Add a slice of raw serrano chile to each panucho just before folding it in half.

LOBSTER, CHAYOTE, AND MANGO TOSTADAS
WITH CHIPOTLE CREMA

Serves 6. Tostada is the generic name for tortilla chips; it is also the name given to small round corn tortillas that have been fried crisp and topped with something juicy and saucy. This sophisticated and fresh-tasting lobster "salsa" balances sweet lobster meat, spicy chipotle, and fresh mango with a touch of crisp, pale-green chayote. The tostadas should be freshly fried and sprinkled with a little ground chile and salt, or try the low-fat tostada method (page 85). Shrimp or fresh Dungeness crab may be substituted for the lobster.

¼ cup thick Mexican crema or sour cream

3 teaspoons finely chopped chipotles in adobo, or more to taste

2 teaspoons fresh-squeezed orange juice

Kosher salt

6-ounce Maine lobster tail, raw

1 tablespoon olive oil

½ cup chayote, peeled and cut into ¼-inch dice

1 tablespoon minced white onion

¼ cup firm, ripe mango, peeled and cut into ¼-inch dice

1 tablespoon fresh-squeezed lime juice, or to taste

1 tablespoon chopped cilantro

Warm tostadas

1 tablespoon ground California or ancho chile

Garnish: 16 perfect cilantro leaves

1. Combine the crema, chipotles, orange juice, and ¼ teaspoon salt. Set aside.

2. Remove the lobster from the shell, devein it, and cut it into ¼-inch dice.

3. Heat the olive oil in a sauté pan over medium-high heat. Add the chayote and onions and cook, stirring occasionally, until lightly browned. Add the lobster meat and season with salt to taste. Cook, stirring, until the lobster is cooked through. Remove from heat and cool 5 minutes, then stir in the diced mango, lime juice, and cilantro. (At this point the mixture may be refrigerated for up to 2 hours, loosely covered.)

4. To serve, sprinkle ground ancho chile and salt over the warm tostadas. Spoon some of the lobster mixture on each one, then a teaspoon or more of the chipotle crema, and garnish with a cilantro leaf.

PAPAS LOCAS
(ROASTED STUFFED POTATOES)

Makes 6 potatoes. Every pueblo has intrepid potato vendors who heed the call for something different from the usual run of street food. For each order, the vendor cracks open a hot, foil-wrapped potato that has been baked in the coals of a wood fire. He mixes the steaming, fluffy insides with diced carne asada, pieces of butter, a good pinch of onions, and cubes of cheese—usually Jack, but queso fresco or cotixa are other choices. The potato, now almost completely *loca*, is rewrapped and popped back into the embers for several minutes, until it is piping hot. The diner finishes the papa loca with pico de gallo, pickled jalapeños, and whatever else the stand might offer for garnishes—tasty bits like tart Mexican sour cream (*crema*), ground chiles, chicharrón (crispy pork rinds), cilantro, green onions, chipotle salsa . . . the list goes on and on.

6 small russet baking potatoes

1 tablespoon olive oil

Kosher salt

Half recipe carne asada (page 107), cooked and diced

1½ cups grated Jack cheese

1 stick salted butter, cut into 6 pieces

1 small white onion, peeled and cut into small dice

To serve: sliced pickled jalapeños, pico de gallo (page 128), assorted salsas and garnishes as desired

1. Preheat the oven to 400 degrees. Thoroughly scrub the potatoes with a stiff brush and dry them with a towel. Rub the outsides with olive oil and a sprinkling of kosher salt. Wrap each one in a foil square. Bake for 45 minutes, or until cooked through.

2. Unwrap the potatoes carefully, split them open, and break up the insides slightly with a fork. Inside each potato, mix together some diced carne asada, 2 tablespoons shredded cheese, a cube of butter, and finally, a couple of tablespoons of onion. Sprinkle with salt. Close the potato up as best you can, rewrap it, and return it to the oven for 10 minutes.

3. Serve the potatoes with the jalapeños, the pico de gallo, and any other toppings that catch your fancy.

SPICY MASA

Makes about 18 masa balls. Chef Jesús Gonzáles introduced me to this recipe at the Rancho La Puerta resort in Tecate, Mexico. Fresh corn masa is easy to make and use, and it has applications far beyond simple tortillas, in all kinds of stuffed and rolled snacks. Not only that, it is infinitely adaptable to flavors; for example, try adding a pinch of ground ancho chile, or substituting minced green onion tops for the jalapeños, or adding a few sesame seeds to the mix.

2 cups Maseca brand masa harina for tortillas

1½ to 2 cups warm water

¼ teaspoon salt

1 tablespoon finely minced seeded jalapeño

1 teaspoon finely minced garlic

1. In a bowl, combine the masa harina, 1½ cups water, and the salt. Work the masa with your hands to form a soft dough. Work in the jalapeño and garlic.

2. To test the consistency of the masa, form a small ball and press it flat. If it cracks around the edges, add more water as needed, a little at a time. The dough should be very soft but not wet. Form into balls the size of a golf ball and cover until ready to use. If the dough begins to crack while you are working with it, dip 2 fingers into water and work it into the dough ball; do not pour water directly into the dough.

MORE GARNISHES FOR PAPAS LOCAS

- Shrimp sautéed with garlic
- Crumbled bacon
- Chopped fresh garlic
- Cooked Mexican chorizo
- Hot-smoked fish
- Roasted serrano chiles
- Mushrooms with garlic and epazote
- Anchovies
- Crumbled blue cheese
- Sliced or grilled scallions
- Rajas (page 92)

PAN-ROASTED GÜERO CHILES
WITH BLACKENED ONIONS

Makes 12 chiles. Fresh chiles are so basic to Mexican cooking that it's easy to over-look them as a treat in their own right. All chiles do not taste alike; pale yellow güero chiles (the name means "blond" and is often applied to Americans or light-haired Mexicans) have a pleasantly assertive flavor. The simple technique of pan-roasting them brings out their fruitiness and makes for a delicious nibble or side dish. A squeeze of lemon juice adds sweetness, while soy sauce subtly adds color and salti-ness (soy is a frequent, if underplayed, ingredient in many modern Mexican recipes). The recipe may also be prepared with spicier jalapeños, though güeros, too, can be spicy without warning. Small pointed sweet peppers or Japanese shishito peppers are reliably milder substitutes.

1 white onion	2 tablespoons soy sauce
1 tablespoon olive oil	¼ cup water
12 güero chiles, washed, left whole with stems on	½ lemon or lime

1. Peel the onion and trim a good inch from both top and bottom. Cut it in half from top to bottom and slice each half into ¼-inch-wide strips, cutting from end to end. Heat the olive oil in a heavy pan over medium heat. Add the onion and cook, stirring often, until it is soft and deeply caramelized—almost burned. Remove the onions from the pan and add the chiles. Cook the chiles over medium-high heat without turning too often, until they blacken in places.

2. Remove the pan from the heat. Pour the soy sauce over the chiles and shake. Return the pan to the heat and cook until the soy sauce is dry. Then add the water and cook until all the liquid has evaporated, glazing the chiles. Remove the pan from the heat and stir in the onions. Squeeze the lemon over all, and serve the chiles at room temperature.

OCTOPUS SALPICÓN
WITH PEPPERS, CAPERS, AND LEMON

Makes 6. Coastal fishing pueblos often make colorful salpicóns from fresh seafood mixed with onions and chiles, rather than the traditional shredded meat, the style becoming popular throughout Mexico. This salpicón is very pretty, with colorful peppers and strips of red onion in a fresh lemon vinaigrette with slices of sweet, octopus.

- 1 small octopus (about 2 pounds, see note)
- ½ cup thinly sliced red onion
- ½ cup thinly sliced green bell pepper
- ½ cup thinly sliced red bell pepper
- 1 small serrano chile, thinly sliced in rings
- 1 tablespoon capers, rinsed
- 1 teaspoon fresh oregano leaves, minced
- 1 tablespoon fresh garlic, minced

- ½ teaspoon fresh-ground black pepper
- 2 tablespoons peppery extra-virgin olive oil, such as arbequina
- Kosher salt to taste
- 2–3 tablespoons fresh-squeezed lemon juice
- 6 fresh corn tostadas (page 85)
- 1 avocado, diced
- **To serve:** lemon wedges

1. Several hours before serving, cook the octopus: If it is frozen, thaw it under cold running water. Rinse fresh octopus well in cold water. Place it in a 4-quart saucepan and cover with cold water. Bring the water to a boil, reduce the heat, and simmer for 45 minutes to an hour, until the tip of a sharp knife inserted where the tentacle meets the head goes in easily. When tender, transfer it to an ice bath. Drain.

2. Combine the red onion, bell peppers, and serrano in a bowl with the capers, oregano, garlic, black pepper, olive oil, 1 teaspoon of the salt, and 2 tablespoons of the lemon juice.

3. Cut the octopus tentacles into slices less than ¼ inch thick, until you have about 1 cup. Combine with the pepper mixture. Taste for lemon juice or salt. The salpicón is ready to serve; you may cover and refrigerate it for up to 1 hour. Stir well before serving.

4. Place a generous spoonful on a tostada, topped with some diced avocado and a sprinkle of salt. Offer more lemon wedges on the side.

NOTE: If dealing with a whole octopus is too much for you, cooked octopus, called *tako*, is available in the fish section of most Asian markets. You will need about 1 cup of it.

GUACAMOLE CON FRUTAS
(GUACAMOLE WITH FRUIT)

Serves 6. Fruited guacamoles are all the rage in Mexico, and some of the more common versions also include shrimp, chorizo or bacon, strong cheeses, tequilas and smoky mezcals, and unusual herbs such as epazote or licorice-flavored *hoja santa*. Try this surprisingly addictive version, laced with mango, crunchy-tart pomegranate seeds, and tequila, and see if it doesn't turn your idea of guacamole on its head.

2 ripe Hass avocados

1 tablespoon fresh-squeezed lime juice (about 1 lime)

½ teaspoon kosher salt

¼ cup finely diced white onion

¼ cup chopped cilantro

1 serrano chile, minced (optional)

2 tablespoons cored and seeded Roma tomato, diced

2 tablespoons peeled ripe mango, cut into small dice

1 teaspoon blanco tequila

1 teaspoon lime juice

1 tablespoon goat cheese, crumbled

1 tablespoon pomegranate seeds

Garnish: cilantro sprig, fresh tostadas (page 85), lime wedges

1. Split, pit, and mash the avocado flesh with the lime juice and salt, using a potato masher, fork, or a whisk in an up and down motion—never a blender or food processor. Stir in the onion, cilantro, serrano, and tomato. Place in a serving dish.

2. Toss the mango with the tequila and lime juice.

3. Arrange the mango, goat cheese, and pomegranate seed in neat rows on top of the mashed avocado. Set a cilantro sprig on top and serve with fresh tostadas and limes. At the table, stir the ingredients into the guacamole and enjoy.

VARIATION: If fresh pomegranates are not available, substitute toasted pine nuts.

SCALLOP AGUACHILES
IN VOLCANO SAUCE

Serves 6. I first tasted this bright green aguachiles in Cabo San Lucas at bustling Taqueria Rossy, where it was made with small local scallops just a few hours out of the water. Aguachiles is simply raw shellfish, always sweet and fresh (usually shrimp or scallops, but any very fresh seafood may be used), combined with a vivid sauce and crunchy vegetables just before serving. It is even less "cooked" than ceviche. As the name warns, this aguachiles is very spicy, and for maximum heat and freshest flavor, it should be made just before you need it. Combine the seafood and salsa immediately before serving. The scallops cure before your eyes. Look for untreated or dry-pack scallops, which are naturally firm and sweet.

1 hothouse cucumber

½ red onion

6 medium tomatillos

2–4 large jalapeños (depending on your chile tolerance)

1 cup packed cilantro, leaves and small stems only (about 1 medium bunch)

1½ teaspoons kosher salt

1 pound very fresh, dry-pack (untreated) scallops

¼ cup fresh-squeezed lime juice

¼ cup julienned red bell pepper

Warm corn tostadas (page 85)

1. Peel the cucumber, trim both ends, halve it lengthwise, and cut it into very thin slices. Peel the onion, trim the top and bottom, and cut it into paper-thin slices.

2. Husk and wash the tomatillos, and cut them into quarters. Stem the jalapeños and cut them into several pieces without removing the seeds. Place half of the jalapeño pieces in a food processor with the tomatillos, cilantro, and salt. Puree to a smooth, bright-green sauce, scraping the sides of the bowl several times. Taste for heat—the sauce should be very spicy—and add more jalapeños as needed.

3. Pat the scallops dry and remove the fibrous muscle from the sides. Cut each scallop into slices about ¼ inch thick. Toss the scallops with the lime juice so they are coated on all sides. Combine the salsa with the onions and cucumbers, then fold in the scallops.

4. Serve right away in a chilled bowl, with the julienne red pepper scattered on top and tostadas on the side. If the aguachiles will be on a buffet, set the serving bowl on ice.

NOTE: If you prefer not to eat raw seafood, the scallops may be briefly cooked and chilled before being combined in step 3.

MEXICAN HOT DOG
WITH CHIPOTLE KETCHUP

Makes 6 dogs. The infamous *perro caliente* has a devoted, even fanatical, following. It is a product of that uneasy netherworld between processed foods and ancient traditions that now exists in every culinary culture and has spawned such aberrations as spushi—sushi made with Spam—and hot dog ceviche. But this truly noble concoction will lift you to heights that sauerkraut and onions can only dream of attaining. Imagine a dog wrapped in bacon, then fried; enfolded in a warm, squishy garlic-toasted roll; topped with lime mayonnaise, spicy pico de gallo, and chipotle-spiked ketchup; and mounded with pickled jalapeños, cilantro sprigs, and white onions. I would walk over hot coals, any day, for one of these.

1–4 canned chipotles in adobo

¾ cup ketchup

6 hot dogs

6 strips of thinly sliced, inexpensive bacon

¼ cup mayonnaise

2 cloves garlic, smashed to a smooth paste

6 hot dog rolls

Mayonesa sauce (page 130)

Pico de gallo (page 128)

Sliced pickled jalapeños

½ cup diced white onions or grilled onions

6 leafy cilantro sprigs

1. Puree the chipotles with the ketchup, using the number of chiles that suits your taste and tolerance for heat. Set aside. (You may also substitute any Mexican hot sauce.)

2. Wrap each hot dog with a strip of bacon and secure with a toothpick. Fry the hot dogs slowly in a sauté pan over medium heat until the bacon is well-cooked and crisp. The bacon should render enough fat as you cook, but you may add a little oil or butter to the pan, if you like.

3. While the hot dogs are cooking, mix the mayonnaise with the garlic paste and spread it lightly on the inside of the rolls. Heat another frying pan or griddle, and toast the buns, mayonnaise side down, until browned and crisp inside. Keep warm.

4. Remove and discard the toothpicks from the hot dogs and place each one in a roll. Top each to taste with mayonesa sauce, chipotle ketchup, pico de gallo, jalapeños, onions, and cilantro.

SALMON CEVICHE
WITH GINGER, APPLE, AND CUCUMBER

Serves 6. Ceviche originated in Peru, where it is still very simple—raw seafood with a few chiles and other vegetables, tossed with fresh-squeezed citrus juice just before serving. (Ceviche is not cooked with heat, so using fresh, top-quality fish is essential.) In theory, any raw fish can be cured in citrus, combined with almost anything, and still be called "ceviche." Chefs can, and do, go wild elaborating on this basic idea, using all types of seafood, and adding everything from caviar to coconut to potatoes. (Some even add a dash of tequila or other liquor, such as gin or vodka.) I love this simple preparation. While it doesn't stray too far from the classic recipe, the balance of ginger and chile is an exciting change, especially with a hint of sweetness from the apple. Wild salmon is an excellent choice for ceviche, especially colorful, fatty sockeye, which turns an even brighter coral color in the citrus bath. Don't leave the fish in too long, though, or it will lose its delicacy.

12 ounces best-quality, very fresh wild sockeye salmon or other wild salmon (see note)

Kosher salt

4–5 tablespoons fresh-squeezed lime juice

4 tablespoons fresh-squeezed lemon juice

2 teaspoons minced fresh ginger

1 tablespoon minced serrano chile

Half a medium cucumber, peeled, seeded, and cut into ¼-inch dice (about ¾ cup)

1 Roma tomato, cored and cut into ¼-inch dice

⅓ cup red onion, cut into ¼-inch dice

¼ cup tart green apple, peeled and cut into ¼-inch dice

⅓ cup cilantro leaves, chopped

Warm corn tostadas (page 85)

1. Remove the skin and any bones from the salmon and cut it into small cubes, about ⅜ inch square. Place the cubes in a glass bowl and stir in 1½ teaspoons of the salt, 4 teaspoons of the lime juice, the lemon juice, ginger, and minced chiles. Cover and refrigerate for 15 to 30 minutes.

2. Stir in the remaining ingredients, taste for salt and lime, and add more if needed. Serve right away with crisp tostadas.

NOTE: Fresh wild salmon has a limited season, but this ceviche can also be made successfully with good-quality frozen wild salmon—just make sure it is American-caught, too. Many foreign fisheries are neither sustainable nor well managed, and some salmon populations are endangered by overfishing.

VARIATIONS:

- ✤ As always, you may adjust the amount of hot chiles to your liking, or leave them out altogether.

- ✤ Try using diced mango in place of the apple.

- ✤ Serve the ceviche on cucumber slices.

El flojo trabaja doble.

The lazy man works twice as hard.

CEVICHE MACHO

(RAW BEEF CEVICHE WITH JICAMA, LIME, & HABANERO)

Serves 6. Technically, ceviche is made of seafood—but the basic concept lends itself to many unusual combinations. This unusual antojito is not for the faint of heart. Not only are you eating raw meat, but the ceviche is loaded with onions and *very* spicy. Feeling macho? Habaneros are the hottest chiles available, and definitely not for those with low tolerance. You can, of course, substitute jalapeño or serrano chiles, but the dish will lose some of its over-the-top appeal.

This looks more like a Mexican beef tartare than a ceviche, since the beef is not in the lime juice long enough for the color to change much. Keep the ceviche very cold, and eat it right away, while the beef is still raw. Knock this back with an ice-cold beer, a good tequila, or both. (It's also very tasty with a glass of frozen vodka.) Follow with a big cigar.

10 ounces very lean, fresh beef (filet, top round, or sirloin, preferably a premium grass-fed brand)

Kosher salt

½ small habanero chile, seeded and minced (less than 1 teaspoon, see note)

1 cup seeded, diced Roma tomatoes

1 cup diced red onion

½ jicama, peeled and cut into small dice, about 1 cup

2 tablespoons chopped cilantro

5–6 tablespoons fresh-squeezed lime juice, or to taste

Warm corn tostadas (recipe follows)

½ avocado, diced

Flake sea salt

1. Trim all visible fat and sinew from the beef and cut it into ⅜ inch dice. You should have about 8 ounces of meat after cleaning. Mix with ½ teaspoon salt and the chopped chiles. Chill for 1 hour.

2. Combine the tomatoes, onion, jicama, and cilantro with 5 tablespoons of the lime juice and another ½ teaspoon salt. Chill for 30 minutes.

3. Just before serving, combine the beef and tomato salsa. Taste for seasoning (you may want to add more lime juice and salt). The mixture will be very spicy.

4. Heap the ceviche onto the tostadas and top with diced avocado. Sprinkle a few crystals of crunchy sea salt on the avocado.

NOTE: Wearing disposable gloves is a good idea when handling any hot chile, but it is *especially* important with habaneros.

CORN TOSTADAS

Makes 48. Classic tostadas, crisp and delicious.

Vegetable oil for frying

Kosher salt

1 dozen stale corn tortillas, quartered

1. Heat about ¾ inch of vegetable oil in a heavy sauté pan over medium-high heat. (Set the pan on a back burner, for safety). Line a plate with paper towels or set a rack over a second pan.

2. When the oil is hot, fry the tortillas a few at a time until they are crisp and golden brown. Drain them well and sprinkle them while still warm with a little kosher salt. Serve immediately.

LOW-FAT TOSTADAS

Makes 48. Baked tostadas will be a bit sturdier than fried, but they are still crisp and tasty, perfect for piling on the goodies.

1 dozen stale corn tortillas

Kosher salt

About ¼ cup vegetable or olive oil

1. Preheat the oven to 350 degrees. Line a baking sheet with parchment paper or a nonstick silicone mat.

2. Brush the tortillas lightly on both sides with the oil, then place the tortillas in a stack. Cut the stacked tortillas into quarters.

3. Arrange the pieces in one layer on the baking sheet, without overlapping. Sprinkle them lightly with salt.

4. Bake for 20 to 30 minutes, or until lightly browned and very crisp.

NOTE: Any leftovers may be reheated until crisp.

CHAPTER 3

TACOS

Come y calla.

Eat and shut up.

Tacos are not a serious meal, but they are taken very seriously in Mexico, where even the most humble taco stand is plastered with signs proclaiming that there are to be found tacos *ricos*, tacos *super-fantasticos*, tacos *los mejores del mundo*. Humility is clearly not part of the recipe for a great taco. What is essential are freshness and character—delivering big flavors in small bites.

You need never be without a taco in Mexico. In the morning, stands offer meltingly tender braised meats, juicy and savory with chile and tomato—a perfect morning pick-me-up. At midday the streets fill with the wonderful smells of grilling carne asada and chickens smoke-roasting over wood, rotisseries loaded with pork *al pastor* and *discas* bubbling away with crisp fish and shrimp for tacos.

The cheerful anarchy of the street rewards taco makers who treat their calling as an art, whose culinary performance, good or bad, is honest—carried out an arm's length from the customer. There is no hiding, no fixing, no fudging, no *fluff*. Like great chefs, fearless *taqueros* are always evolving, nicking ideas from anyone and anything. The taco is the perfect vehicle for experimentation because, really, anything goes in a taco so long as it fits on a tortilla, can be eaten standing up without implements, and is delicious.

The tacos in this chapter were inspired by great ideas from both sides of the border. While many flavors are traditional, you will see that some of the techniques and combinations take the typical taco up to the edge—and occasionally over it. An amusing trend is the Iron Law of Escalation: A taco may always be made larger, hotter, gooier, or with more goodies on top. But it's all in good fun.

TACOS 101

HOW TO WARM A TORTILLA

Prepare a tortilla basket lined with a napkin or a double layer of foil that can be folded over itself. Heat a heavy, ungreased pan or comal until very hot, almost smoking. Lay a couple of tortillas in the pan, press gently for several seconds, then turn them and heat the other side. The tortillas are ready when they are soft and pliable. Stack the tortillas in the prepared basket and fold the napkin or foil, over to keep them warm and steaming while you heat the remaining tortillas.

CORN OR FLOUR?

Taco stand tacos are always made on fresh corn tortillas; flour tortillas are eaten in restaurants and at home. To me, the rich taste of corn masa is an integral part of the flavor of any taco. You may use either corn or flour in any of the taco recipes, according to your preference.

SALSAS & GARNISHES

❖ Salsas add that final hit of freshness and color. They should always be well seasoned and powerfully flavored.

❖ Always offer a couple of tomato or chile salsas, one hot and one mild, and a creamy-textured pureed sauce such as Avocado Cilantro Sauce (page 130) or Chipotle Salsa (page 138) to add moisture.

❖ Acidic salsas, such as Salsa Verde made with tomatillos (page 135), are essential with rich meats like pork and tongue.

❖ Garnishes add crunch, color, and yet another shot of flavor. Typical garnishes might include: Diced white onions (sometimes mixed with chopped cilantro, cilantro sprigs, cut limes, kosher salt, radishes, pickled onions and jalapeño, Bottled hot sauce (Salsa Huichol or Salsa Amor)

TACO RULES

1. Take a little bit of everything, but try not overfill your taco or it may burst. (This does not contradict the Iron Law of Escalation.)

2. Hold the taco with both hands while eating it, and place your little finger over the end to keep in the filling.

3. With braised meat tacos, offer a small bowl of the cooking juices for dipping between bites.

SHRIMP TACO DORADO

Makes 12 substantial tacos, enough for 6 hungry people. The *dorado* taco is a supertaco—a new trend in which the basic taco is elaborated upon by adding more salsas, cheese, and garnishes; adding layers; toasting and frying; and generally pushing the taco to its limit. (See also the Taco *Vampiro*, page 107.) A good *dorado* is gooey, substantial, and filling—a corn tortilla fried on the griddle with a little butter or oil until golden and half crisped, then stuffed with cheese and any number of fillings and sauces.

This taco, a favorite of mine, tops melted cheese with garlicky shrimp, guacamole, and chipotle salsa, then finishes with a spoonful of sweet-hot mango habanero salsa and fresh cilantro sprigs. It all comes together quickly, so make sure everything is ready to serve before you start cooking the shrimp.

1 tablespoon plus 2 teaspoons butter or olive oil

1 teaspoon chopped garlic

1 pound medium shrimp, peeled, tails removed, and cut in half if large

1 teaspoon finely chopped chipotles in adobo

¼ teaspoon salt

Large corn tortillas

1½ cups grated Jack cheese

Chipotle salsa (page 138)

Guacamole (page 77)

Mango habanero salsa (page 136)

Cilantro sprigs

1. In an 8-inch sauté pan, melt 1 tablespoon of the butter or oil over medium heat. When it is heated, but not brown, add the garlic and shrimp, and cook, stirring, until the shrimp are pink. Stir in the chipotles and salt and remove from the heat.

2. Preheat a heavy pan or griddle over medium heat and brush it lightly with some of the remaining butter or olive oil. Set a corn tortilla on the griddle and scatter 2 tablespoons of shredded Jack cheese evenly over the tortilla. Set 3 or 4 shrimp on one side of the tortilla. When the cheese starts to melt, fold the tortilla in half over the shrimp, and continue to cook on both sides until the cheese is melted and the tortilla is lightly crisped and golden brown.

3. Open the taco. Dollop 1 teaspoon of chipotle salsa on top of the shrimp and follow with a tablespoon each of guacamole and mango habanero salsa. Tuck a couple of cilantro sprigs into the opening and serve right away.

GARLIC SHRIMP TACO
WITH POBLANO CHILE RAJAS

Makes 12 tacos. I first tasted a variation of this taco at El Taco de la Ermita in Tijuana, where *taquero* extraordinaire Javier Campos served it *dorado* style with several of his magical salsas. In this simplified version, the delicious, smoky-rich flavor comes from the roasted chiles poblanos. Poblanos are wide and sharply pointed, with dark green, shiny skin. They come into their own when charred and sautéed with onions and garlic into *rajas* (literally, "rags"). Ripe red poblanos, also called for in the recipe, may be found in Latin markets from September to November. If it's not the right season, substitute bell pepper. Note that poblano chiles can be spicy, so if you don't like heat, substitute mild, light-green Anaheims. This is also great over rice.

1 green poblano or Anaheim chile

1 red poblano chile or red bell pepper

2 teaspoons olive oil

3 tablespoons white onion, cut into ½-inch dice

¾ pound medium shrimp, peeled and deveined

½ teaspoon kosher salt

Fresh-ground black pepper

1 teaspoon finely chopped fresh garlic

1 tablespoon unsalted butter, at room temperature

2 teaspoons fresh-squeezed lime juice

1 tablespoon chopped cilantro

To serve: warm corn tortillas, pico de gallo (page 128)

1. Char the whole peppers on all sides, by placing them directly in a gas flame or under a hot broiler. Wrap them in a paper towel and allow to cool completely, then remove the stem and seeds. Rub off the charred skin with the towel—do not wash the chiles or you'll lose all that great smoky flavor. Cut the peppers into ½-inch dice.

2. Heat an 8-inch sauté pan over medium-high heat. Add the oil, then the diced peppers and onion. Cook, stirring, for 2 minutes, until the vegetables are tender and even a little browned.

3. Add the shrimp, season with salt and pepper, and continue to cook, stirring often, until they are pink and firm.

4. Add the chopped garlic and cook for 30 seconds. Remove from heat and stir in the butter until it melts. Add the lime juice and cilantro.

5. Serve right away with warm corn tortillas and pico de gallo.

GRILLED LAMB TACO
WITH SALSA BORRACHA AND SALSA VERDE

Makes 12 large tacos. *Birria de chivo* is a beloved traditional street food, usually eaten early in the day or for lunch, along with a bowl of beans and some radishes and onions. Big chunks of lamb or goat meat are rubbed with a spice blend (the recipe for which is always guarded by the family), then slowly simmered until tender with chiles and tomatoes. The meat is removed from the broth, then roasted, shredded, and served with a tequila-laced sauce and plenty of tortillas for dipping. It's delicious, but the lengthy cooking process (not to mention finding a goat) can be daunting.

This quick variation on the idea echoes the flavors of birria but speeds up the process considerably by using spice-rubbed boneless lamb, given a quick turn on the grill. Serve slivers of the juicy pink meat with tequila-laced salsa borracha, rich with dried chile flavor, and pale-green salsa verde, a sprightly tomatillo-avocado mix. The lamb tacos taste great with black beans on the side.

1 pound lamb loin or lamb sirloin

2 tablespoons olive oil

1½ teaspoons kosher salt

1 tablespoon minced garlic

1 teaspoon minced fresh ginger

1 teaspoon ground ancho chile

1 teaspoon ground California or guajillo chile

2 teaspoons ground chipotle chile

½ teaspoon unsweetened cocoa powder

12 warm corn tortillas

Diced white onions mixed with chopped cilantro

To serve: salsa verde (page 135), salsa borracha (page 132), black beans (optional, page 140)

1. With a sharp knife, remove all the fat and silverskin from the lamb. Cut the meat into several smaller pieces to expose more surface to the marinade.

2. Combine the oil, salt, garlic, and ginger to make a paste. Stir in the ground chiles and cocoa, and rub the mixture into the lamb. Refrigerate, covered, for several hours.

3. Heat a grill or grill pan over medium-high heat and grill the lamb to medium-rare, 3 to 5 minutes per side. Let the meat rest briefly on a warm plate, uncovered.

4. Slice or dice the lamb, pile it onto the tortillas, and top each taco with a sprinkle of the onion-and-cilantro mix. Serve the salsas on the side, along with the beans, if desired.

TACO DE LECHUGA
WITH PILONCILLO BBQ SHRIMP

Makes 12 tacos. I've seen some wild variations on the taco theme (foie gras tacos, raw food tacos, s'mores taco cookies, and deep-fried tacos as big as plates, for example), so I'm open-minded about what makes a taco a taco, as long as all works in my mouth. Here, instead of the expected tortilla, the sweet-spicy shrimp mixture is rolled up in crisp lettuce leaves with plenty of onion and cilantro. This is a great recipe to make for a group or set out for a party, with the lettuce and garnishes alongside. The balance of heat and sweet in the sauce contrasts delightfully with the cool, crisp lettuce wrappers. The same sauce is good on grilled pork or chicken.

1 small head iceberg lettuce

¾ cup finely diced white onion

¼ cup chopped cilantro

2 teaspoons olive oil

1 pound medium shrimp, peeled and cut into 2 or 3 pieces each

1 large Roma tomato, cored and diced

½ teaspoon salt

Piloncillo BBQ sauce (recipe follows)

1 tablespoon unsalted butter, at room temperature

Sliced pickled jalapeños

1. From the bottom, cut the center core out of the lettuce and carefully separate the head into individual leaves. Wash well, pat dry, and place in a sealed plastic bag. Chill until ready to use. (Ideally, the leaves should be crisp, but flexible.) Stir together ½ cup of the diced onion and the chopped cilantro and set aside.

2. Heat the olive oil in a 10-inch sauté pan over medium heat. Add the shrimp all at once and cook, stirring, until they are firm and pink, about 2 minutes. Add the remaining onion and the diced tomato and cook 1 minute longer. Season with the salt.

3. Add ¾ cup of the BBQ sauce (reserve the remainder to use when assembling the tacos) and simmer until it is slightly thickened and clings to the shrimp. Remove the pan from the heat and stir the butter into the sauce until thoroughly combined.

4. To serve, place a few shrimp and some BBQ sauce on a lettuce leaf. Top with the onion-and-cilantro mixture and a few pickled jalapeño slices. Roll up and enjoy.

PILONCILLO BBQ SAUCE

Makes about 1 cups.

2 teaspoons olive oil

¼ white onion, peeled and diced

1 clove garlic, peeled and chopped

1–2 large chipotle chiles in adobo, roughly chopped

2 tablespoons crushed piloncillo sugar (about 1½ ounces), or firmly packed dark brown sugar

2 Roma tomatoes, cut into eighths

¼ cup water

¼ cup tomato sauce

3–4 teaspoons white vinegar

Kosher salt

1. Heat the olive oil in a medium sauté pan over medium heat. Add the onion and cook, stirring often, until it is soft but not brown. Add the garlic and cook 1 minute longer.

2. Add 1 of the chipotles, the piloncillo, and the tomatoes. Cook, stirring often, until the tomatoes are soft and the sugar almost melted, about 3 minutes. Add the water, tomato sauce, 1 tablespoon of the vinegar, and ½ teaspoon salt, and simmer over low heat for 5 minutes. Transfer the sauce to a blender and pulse several times to puree— leave a little bit of texture.

3. Taste the sauce. If it is too sweet for your taste, add the remaining 1 teaspoon vinegar and another pinch of salt. If you want more heat, add the second chipotle and puree briefly.

GRILLED FISH TACO ZARANDEADO

Makes 12 tacos. Whole grilled fish *zarandeado* is a specialty of the beautiful state of Sinaloa, which faces the Gulf of California and Pacific Ocean. A whole fish—usually some kind of local bass, weighing from 3 to 5 pounds—is butterflied and boned, rubbed with an adobo spice paste and adorned with slivered jalapeños and onions. It is then grilled in a flat wire basket over a wood fire and turned several times during the cooking (*zarandear* means "to spin about, shake up, or turn upside down"). When cooked, the whole fish is served skin side down on a piece of rough plank, along with an assortment of salsas, avocado, and tortillas. If you want to tackle it, a whole fish is great fun to grill and looks terrific (maybe for the next PTA potluck?) but using filleted fish is much easier. A grill basket is recommended for cooking the fish; it may also be cooked in a grill pan or sautéed. Make sure to get nice, dark grill marks on the fish, which brings out the flavors of the spice paste.

½ small white onion

4 cloves garlic, peeled and chopped

1 serrano chile, stemmed and chopped

1 teaspoon kosher salt

2 teaspoons olive oil

1 tablespoon achiote paste

1 teaspoon cumin

2 or more teaspoons white vinegar

2 or more teaspoons fresh-squeezed lime juice

1½ pounds farm-raised catfish, striped bass, or other sustainable fish (see sidebar page 99)

1 whole jalapeño, stemmed and thinly sliced

12 warm corn tortillas

Lime wedges

Pineapple cucumber salsa (page 137) or mango habanero salsa (page 136)

Salsa quemada (page 129)

Avocado cilantro sauce (page 130)

Finely shredded green cabbage

1. Make the adobo paste: Chop enough of the onion to make 2 tablespoons and place it in in a *molcajete* or food processor with the garlic and serrano. Sprinkle with salt and grind to a very smooth paste. Mix in the olive oil, achiote paste, and cumin. Add 2 teaspoons each of vinegar and lime juice, then add more as need to make a fairly thick paste.

2. Cut the fish into several large pieces and coat them thickly on all sides with the adobo. Wrap and chill for at least 1 hour.

3. While the fish is marinating, make the salsas and prepare the cilantro sauce, avocado, cilantro sprigs, and lim wedges, and cabbage. Cut ¼ onion from the remaining piece of white onion and slice it thinly (reserve any onion left over for another use).

4. Heat a grill or grill pan to medium-hot. Place the fish in a grill basket and press half the jalapeños and sliced onions onto it. Turn the fish over and repeat on the other side. Grill the fish without moving it until it is well cooked on one side, then turn it carefully, trying to keep as much of the spice paste on the fish as possible. If the fish is very thick, you may need to finish cooking it in a 350-degree oven. Transfer the cooked fish to a warmed serving platter.

5. To make a taco, spoon a little avocado cilantro sauce onto a tortilla. Break up the fish and put some on the sauce. Top with a squeeze of lime, a small amount of each salsa, and some shredded cabbage.

VARIATION: Purists will enjoy this fish simply topped off with a squeeze of lime, a sprinkle of diced onions and avocado, and a sprig of cilantro.

SUSTAINABLE SEAFOOD

Many wild fish are in danger of extinction due to over fishing and pollution. All these recipes may be made with a sustainable fish such as American farmed catfish or striped bass. To learn more about this important issue, see the Monterey Bay Aquarium's Seafood Watch initiative (www.montereybayaquarium.org/cr/seafoodwatch.aspx) or the Marine Stewardship Council (msc.com).

TACO GOBERNADOR, TIJUANA STYLE
(GOVERNOR'S SMOKED FISH TACO)

Makes 6 tacos. Tijuana's seafood restaurants are as good as any in Mexico. This smoked fish taco with melted cheese and a pink sauce is popular in the Tijuana area, owing perhaps to the fact that smoked fish was once a staple of the local diet. Western Baja California, with its hundreds of miles of Pacific coastline, is famous for smoked fish made from huge game fish such as marlin and tuna. The original "governor's taco" (so-named because of its luxurious ingredients) is thought to have originated in Sinaloa, where it is most often made with fresh shrimp. Shrimp are a Gulf catch, and before there was good transportation across the Peninsula, they were a rarity—thus the smoked fish substitution. When you make your taco, be generous with the sauce—smoked fish is dry—and pile on the onions and cilantro.

Vegetable oil, for the giddle

6 large corn tortillas

6 ounces grated Oaxaca or Jack cheese

6 ounces firm-textured, hot-smoked marlin or other hot-smoked fish, such as albacore, broken into pieces

Salsa gobernador (recipe follows)

Pico de gallo (page 128)

Salsa de chiles de arbol (page 131) or bottled hot sauce (optional)

Diced white onion (optional)

Cilantro sprigs (optional)

1. Heat a large griddle or *comal* and brush it generously with oil.

2. Lay the tortillas flat on the griddle, working in batches if necessary, and divide the cheese among them. Top with the smoked fish, fold the tortillas in half, and cook on both sides until the cheese is melted and the tortillas are starting to crisp.

3. Open the tacos and add a dollop with salsa gobernador and pico de gallo. Add hot sauce, onion, and cilantro, if desired.

SALSA GOBERNADOR

Makes scant ½ cup.

¼ cup mayonnaise
2 tablespoons ketchup
Squeeze of fresh lime
Pinch of salt

Combine all the ingredients.

Si quires el perro,
acepta las pulgas.

If you wanted the dog, don't complain
about the fleas.

DEEP-FRIED FISH TACO *CAPEADO*
WITH SPICY COLESLAW

Makes 12 tacos. Fish taco stands dot the roadsides and street corners of northern Baja, and it's hard to pass any of them up. The stands are invariably run by a pair of women (often sisters) who make their own special batters and salsas. Local feelings always run high about whose fish taco is the best, but they are pretty much all the same (and all delicious): beer-battered and fried fish that you top with shredded cabbage, lime-spiked mayonnaise sauce, green avocado sauce, pico de gallo, lime, and hot sauce, all self-served from bowls on the counter of the taco stand. While I do love a traditional fish taco, I also like this twist on the old standard, which uses a tempura-beer batter that fries up crisp and brown. The fish is then set on guacamole with serrano-spiked cabbage slaw in a zippy citrus dressing, and topped with a lush mango habanero salsa. It's important to prepare all the sauces and garnishes ahead; you can refrigerate them until serving time. (Toss the slaw with its dressing just before serving too.) Make sure everything is well-seasoned.

¾ pound farmed fish fillets (see note)

Tempura batter mix

1 bottle ice-cold beer

1 teaspoon dried Mexican oregano, rubbed to a powder

½ teaspoon granulated garlic

½ teaspoon cayenne

¼ teaspoon fresh-ground black pepper

Vegetable oil for deep-frying

½ teaspoon kosher salt

Warm corn tortillas

Guacamole (page 77)

Mayonesa sauce (page 130)

Mango habanero salsa (page 136)

Spicy coleslaw (recipe follows) or shredded green cabbage

Cilantro sprigs

To serve: lime wedges

1. Cut the fish into finger-sized strips and pat dry.

2. Prepare the tempura mix according to the box directions, substituting beer for the liquid. Stir the oregano into the batter along with the cayenne and black pepper. Don't overmix; tempura batter should be lumpy.

3. Heat about 1 inch of oil in a deep pan over medium heat (a wok works perfectly) to 350 degrees on a deep-fry thermometer. (To test the heat, drop a little of the batter in

the oil. When bubbles form quickly all around, the oil is ready.) Dip the fish strips into the tempura batter, allow the excess to drip off, and fry the fish a few pieces at a time until golden brown and very crisp. Sprinkle the fish with the salt, and keep it warm.

4. On a warm corn tortilla, place a spoonful of guacamole, a piece of fish, and drizzle a stripe of mayonesa sauce on top. Top with pico de gallo, coleslaw, and cilantro sprigs. Serve the lime wedges on the side.

NOTE: Either American farm-raised catfish or striped bass are good sustainable choices for fish tacos.

SPICY COLESLAW

Makes 5 cups coleslaw. Don't serve soggy slaw—this one needs to be crisp and fresh to add zip to your tacos. You can prepare the vegetables ahead of time, make the dressing separately, and toss with salad a few minutes before serving.

3 cups thinly sliced green cabbage

1 cup thinly sliced red cabbage

½ cup grated carrot

½ serrano or—for less heat—jalapeño chile, stemmed and minced (about 1 tablespoon)

2 tablespoons minced red bell pepper

½ cup minced red onion

1 bunch cilantro, chopped (about ½ cup)

1 tablespoon fresh-squeezed lime juice

2 tablespoons fresh-squeezed lemon juice

2 tablespoons rice vinegar

2 tablespoons olive oil

½ teaspoon salt

1. In a bowl, combine the cabbages, carrot, chile, bell pepper, onion, and cilantro. In a separate bowl, stir together the remaining ingredients to make the dressing. Just before serving, toss the dressing into the vegetables and use quickly.

COCA-COLA
SHREDDED BEEF TACO

Makes 12 generous tacos. I'm truly shameless when it comes to shaking down other cooks for recipes. It's worth it just for the surprising little tricks I learn, of which this is a prime example. A number of years ago, I was pestering a nice Mexican lady for the recipe for her dark, savory shredded beef, when she nonchalantly mentioned that she added Coca-Cola to the cooking liquid. I've heard many times since about the use of this "secret ingredient" in various recipes, from cakes to salad dressing to BBQ sauces. Mexican Coca-Cola definitely tastes different from American Coke—richer, sweeter, and more complex, possibly due to the use of cane sugar instead of high-fructose corn syrup—but American Coke works fine. The flavor and dark color certainly add something special to this delicious broth, which is not sweet at all, but full of the flavor of dried chiles and tomatoes. Try to buy the beef chuck roast in a single thick piece, which will stay moister than small, thin pieces.

TIP: When you are enjoying a taco of shredded meat, be sure to dip it into the rich braising juices before each bite.

1 tablespoon lard or olive oil	Kosher salt
¼ cup diced onion	1½ cups water
2 large cloves garlic, peeled and sliced	2 pounds chuck roast
3 medium ancho chiles, seeded and stemmed	1½ cups Mexican-bottled Coca-Cola (cane-sugar sweetened)
2 large guajillo chiles, seeded and stemmed	1 bay leaf
½ teaspoon cumin seed	Warm corn or flour tortillas
1 cup canned diced tomatoes	Diced white onion
1 teaspoon dried Mexican oregano	Diced avocado, lightly salted
	Cilantro sprigs

1. In a heavy 2-quart saucepan, heat half the lard or olive oil. Sauté the onion and garlic for 1 minute. Tear the cleaned chiles into pieces, add them to the pan, and cook over medium heat, stirring often, until the onions are soft. Add the cumin seed, diced tomatoes, oregano, 1 teaspoon salt, and the water. Simmer slowly for 20 minutes, or until the chiles are softened. Puree the sauce in a blender until very smooth.

2. Heat the remaining lard in the same pan. Cut the beef into several large chunks and brown it on all sides. Remove it from the pan.

3. Pour the sauce into the pan and cook it, stirring constantly, for several minutes. Return the meat to the sauce. Pour the Coca-Cola into the blender jar, swirl to dissolve any sauce still clinging to the sides, and add it to the pot. Add the bay leaf. Cover the pan, reduce the heat, and simmer until the beef is tender, about 1½ hours.

4. Cool the beef in its cooking liquid for 20 minutes, then transfer it to a cutting board and shred or cut it into ½-inch pieces. Simmer the sauce until it is slightly thickened, another 5 minutes or so, stirring often. Taste and add more salt if desired. Remove the bay leaf.

5. Toss the meat with the sauce to moisten it and roll it up in warm tortillas with diced onions, avocado, and cilantro. Serve very hot, with more sauce on the side.

HANDLING CHILES

The spicy heat in chiles comes from a chemical called capsaicin, and is mostly located in the seeds and ribs. For flavor with less heat, remove them. Generally speaking, the smaller and narrower the chile, the hotter it will be; and a chile with more seeds will be hotter than one with fewer seeds. The chile will be hotter at the stem, where seeds cluster. Always wear gloves when handling any potentially hot chile.

CARNE ASADA TACO VAMPIRO

Makes 12 very substantial tacos. Carne asada is really *the* street taco. Smoky meat, fresh salsas, crunchy onions . . . it just doesn't get any better. Unless, of course, you take it to the next level with a vampiro, a large and succulent example of the supertaco so fabulously good that you'll wish you could eat a dozen. Basically, the vampiro is a chile quesadilla wrapped around juicy grilled carne asada and topped with creamy guacamole, a dash of chipotle salsa, pico de gallo, and salty cotixa cheese. It's fantastic.

Why *vampiro*? Maybe because this taco deserves to be immortal—or because it has a steak through its heart? In Mexico, this marriage of quesadilla and taco is also called a quesotaco.

1 pound well-marbled flap meat or skirt steak

24 fresh corn tortillas

Carne asada marinade (recipe follows)

4 ounces grated Jack or Oaxaca cheese (about 2 cups)

4 serrano chiles, thinly sliced

4 green onions, thinly sliced

Guacamole (page 77)

Pico de gallo (page 128)

Chipotle salsa (page 138)

  cup crumbled cotixa cheese

Cilantro sprigs

1. Cut the meat into 6 pieces and toss with the marinade. Refrigerate and let marinate for several hours or overnight. Grill the meat over a hot fire until it is done to your liking; be sure to let one side char. Rest the meat for 10 minutes, then cut it into small dice and keep it warm under aluminum foil.

2. Heat an ungreased heavy griddle or comal. Lay out 6 tortillas and sprinkle the cheese on top. Scatter serrano chiles and green onions over the Jack cheese, then cover each with a second tortilla. Cook on both sides until the cheese is melted.

3. To assemble the tacos, put 1 tablespoon of guacamole on top of each hot quesadilla. Layer on 2 tablespoons of carne asada and top with a spoonful each of pico de gallo and chipotle salsa. Sprinkle over 1 teaspoon grated cotixa cheese and top with a couple of cilantro sprigs. Roll the taco around the filling and secure it with a toothpick. Eat over a plate so you don't lose anything.

CARNE ASADA MARINADE

Makes enough marinade for about 1 pound of meat.

- 2 tablespoons olive oil
- 1 teaspoon kosher salt
- ½ teaspoon fresh-ground black pepper
- 4 cloves garlic, minced
- 1 teaspoon soy sauce

Combine all the ingredients in a small bowl.

Donde hay chorizo colgando no faltan gatos husmeando.

Where there is sausage hanging, there will be cats sniffing.

CHICKEN-FRIED STEAK TACO
WITH CHILE LIME SAUCE

Makes 12 generous tacos. I'd had so many variations on breaded, crumbed, and battered seafood tacos that I began to wonder why there wasn't a chicken nugget taco, and that line of thought led me to that Texan staple, the chicken-fried steak. It's a logical leap from the traditional fried fish taco, and more to the point, it is delicious: crunchy, spicy, and creamy—a great example of familiar ingredients coming together to make something new. For a truly indulgent treat, add a slice of avocado.

10 ounces flap or skirt steak

Carne asada marinade (page 108)

½ cup all-purpose flour

1 teaspoon salt

½ teaspoon fresh-ground black pepper

2 eggs, beaten

¾ cup panko crumbs (see note)

Vegetable oil, for frying

Spicy chili lime sauce (page 139)

Warm corn tortillas

2 cups shredded iceberg lettuce

2 green onions, sliced crosswise

Cilantro sprigs

Sliced avocado, lightly salted (optional)

1. Cut the meat into pieces the size of your index finger, being careful to cut across the grain. Marinate in the carne asada mixture for 1 hour.

2. Combine the flour, salt, and pepper in a bowl. Pour the egg into a small bowl and the panko into a shallow dish.

3. Heat ½ inch of oil in an 8-inch sauté pan over medium-high heat. Dust each piece of meat in the seasoned flour, then dip it into the egg. Let the excess drip off then roll the meat in the panko crumbs to thoroughly coat.

4. Fry the meat in batches and do not crowd the pan: Gently set each piece separately in the hot oil and cook it until well browned on all sides. As the pieces are done, transfer them to paper towels to drain and keep them warm while you fry the rest.

5. Assemble each taco: Set a piece of chicken-fried steak on a tortilla. Spoon spicy chile lime sauce generously over the meat. Top generously with shredded lettuce, and avocado, if you like. Sprinkle with sliced green onions and a few sprigs of cilantro.

NOTE: Panko crumbs, very crisp, small bread crumbs, are available at Asian markets and some supermarkets.

TACOS OF CARNITAS ROASTED
WITH ORANGE, MILK, AND PEPPER

Serves 6 generously. Many years ago, I worked with a cook who introduced me to this method of roasting pork with milk and fresh orange. Jose has long since retired to his little pueblo in Michoacan, but his recipe lives on in my kitchen simply because it so delicious. Pork cooked this way is moist and succulent, sweet from the natural caramelization of the milk, with the slightest hint of orange and black pepper. For an over-the-top garnish, crumble chicharrón (fried pork skin) on the soft roast meat for a porky, crunchy textural contrast. Serve the carnitas with warm corn tortillas, avocado, a crisp raw tomatillo salsa, and plenty of onions and cilantro. If you have access to heirloom pork such as Kurobuta or Berkshire, it's exceptionally delicious—pork the way pork was meant to taste.

3 pounds boneless pork shoulder (butt) or boneless country pork ribs

1 tablespoon lard

½ teaspoon salt

½ orange, well washed

1 cup whole milk

About 2 cups water

½ teaspoon fresh-ground black pepper

Warm corn tortillas

Diced avocado, lightly salted, or avocado cilantro sauce (page 130)

Raw tomatillo salsa (page 133)

Chicharrónes espumas (skin), crumbled

Diced white onion

Cilantro sprigs

1. Preheat the oven to 350 degrees.

2. Cut the pork into 6 or 8 pieces. Melt the lard in a heavy Dutch oven just large enough to hold the meat in one layer. Brown the meat on all sides and season with salt.

3. Squeeze the orange over the meat and toss the rind into the pan. Pour the milk over the meat and add enough water to almost cover the meat. Sprinkle with pepper. Cover tightly with aluminum foil and bake for about 2 hours, until the meat is fork-tender

4. To finish, uncover the meat and break into into largish pieces Remove the orange rind and discard. Roast, uncovered, until most of the liquid has evaporated, about 20 minutes, or until the meat is brown and crisp on the edges.

5. To assemble the tacos, fill a warm tortilla with shredded pork. Top with avocado and salsa, a little of the chicharrón, and finish with generous amounts of onion and cilantro.

NOTE: Mexican markets and some restaurants and *tortillerias* sell freshly fried chicharrón *espumas*, which are light-years better than the bagged ones. Chicharrón make an excellent taco in their own right when cooked until soft with tomatoes and chiles, then served with a sprinkle of cotixa cheese and raw onion.

**Donde hay hambre
no hay pan duro.**

Where there is hunger
there is no old bread.

LENGUA TACOS
WITH TOMATILLO SALSA

Makes 12 tacos, with some meat left over. Lengua (beef tongue) is much loved by Mexicans, who will go out of their way to visit a stand that serves it, but it is alien to most Americans, who will go out of their way to avoid it. Tongue may well be the weirdest thing you will ever have in your kitchen, but it is worth the shock value and the time it takes to cook it—the meat is delicious—rich and tender. The cooking process is lengthy but simple: a long simmer, followed by cooling in the cooking stock, then a thorough trimming. Serve these taco-stand style with a bit of cooking juice, and the traditional garnishes of roasted tomatillo salsa, and raw white onions mixed with cilantro. The recipe yields about 2 pounds of meat after trimming. Any leftovers may be used in a salpicón of fresh bell peppers, onions, and capers tossed with olive oil, salt and a squeeze of lime juice.

1 beef tongue (about 4 pounds)

2 bay leaves

20 whole black peppercorns

6 whole allspice

3 whole cloves

1 white onion, peeled and left whole

2 heads garlic, washed and cut in half crosswise at about the middle

12 warm corn tortillas

Roasted tomatillo salsa (page 134) or salsa verde (page 135)

Diced white onions mixed with chopped cilantro

1. Rinse the tongue and place it in a large pot with water to cover it by several inches. Add the bay leaves, spices, onion, and garlic. Using a heatproof plate to keep the meat underwater, bring the pot to a simmer over medium heat. Cover it and cook for 5 hours, or until very tender when pierced with a knife. Check occasionally while the tongue is cooking to make sure the meat is still submerged in the stock. If necessary, add more water. Set the pot aside so that the tongue can cool in the cooking liquid for 1 hour. Measure 1 cup of the cooking broth and set it aside.

2. Peel the tongue by pulling away the skin, then use a sharp knife to trim the tongue completely on the top and bottom, removing all fat and strange bits.

3. Slice the tongue thinly and keep it warm in the reserved cooking broth while you assemble the tacos. Alternatively, at this point, the meat may be refrigerated in the broth and gently rewarmed when you are ready to serve.

4. Place a portion of meat onto a tortilla, then top it with the salsa and onion-and-cilantro mix.

CHICKEN FAJITA
TACO *DORADO*

Makes 12 large tacos. The fajitas popular today are a fairly recent Tex-Mex invention, based on simple Mexican cowboy food—grilled skirt steak. As good ideas will, fajitas quickly spread across the country (with varying degrees of success), and today chicken is the preferred fajita meat in the United States. Prepared in the pulchritudinous *dorado* style (lightly fried and layered with melted cheese), the chicken is exceptional. The meat stays moist and tender, savory with chiles and garlic, bright with lime and tequila. If you prefer, serve the fajitas alone with warm corn tortillas. For a special treat, prepare this dish as a *vampiro* taco (see page 107), substituting fajitas for carne asada. Of course you can also get back to your *vaquero* roots and make this recipe with beef.

12 ounces boneless, skinless chicken breast or thigh meat

1 tablespoon olive oil

1 teaspoon kosher salt

2 large cloves garlic, peeled and thinly sliced

½ red onion, peeled and cut lengthwise into strips

1 poblano or Anaheim chile, charred, peeled, seeded as for rajas (see page 92), and cut into 1-inch dice

1 red bell pepper, cored and cut into ½-inch dice

½ teaspoon crushed red chiles

½ teaspoon dried Mexican oregano

1 tablespoon blanco tequila

1 tablespoon fresh-squeezed lime juice

1 tablespoon chopped cilantro

Corn tortillas

1 cup shredded Jack cheese

To serve: cilantro sprigs, pickled jalapeño slices, pico de gallo, crumbled cotixa cheese (optional)

1. Cut the chicken into ½-inch cubes. (Freezing the meat for 30 minutes ahead of time makes cutting easier.) Have all the rest of the ingredients prepared and ready at hand.

2. Heat the oil in a heavy sauté pan (preferably cast iron) over medium-high heat. Cook the chicken well, stirring often. Season it with half the salt.

3. Increase the heat to high and add the garlic, onion, fresh peppers, crushed red chiles, and oregano. Cook, stirring constantly, until the vegetables are just wilted, about 3 minutes. Season with the remaining salt. The pan should be almost dry.

4. Remove the pan from the heat and stir in the tequila, lime juice, and chopped cilantro. Keep warm.

5. Lightly butter a large, heavy sauté pan and set it over medium-high heat. Place a corn tortilla in the pan and scatter 1 generous tablespoon of Jack cheese over the top. When the cheese is melted, fill the taco with warm chicken fajitas, fold it in half, and cook a few seconds longer on each side, until the tortilla is half crisp. Serve right away with the cilantro sprigs, jalapeños, pico de gallo, and cotixa cheese, if desired, on the side.

Agua que no has de beber, dejala correr.

If you are not drinking that water, let it run.

BLT CHICKEN TACO

Makes 12 small tacos. Let me stress the importance of using chicken thighs, not breasts, here. Thigh meat is tender, juicy, and more flavorful than breast meat, and often less expensive. It also has plenty of golden fat lurking under the skin, which is rendered out during the cooking process so the skin becomes crisp and the flavor is deepened. The addition of crisp bacon to the taco adds more crunch, salt, and a little smokiness. You'll love the unexpected twists of flavor, especially the combination of crisp chicken skin, smoky bacon, and garlicky aioli. Serve these tacos on small, street-size corn tortillas.

4 large boneless chicken thighs, with skin left on

1 teaspoon olive oil

Kosher salt

¼ cup mayonnaise

2 large cloves garlic, peeled

About 1 teaspoon extra-virgin olive oil

12 (4-inch) corn tortillas, warmed

2 strips bacon, cooked crisp and broken up

4 pickled jalapeños, diced

1 cup shredded lettuce

½ cup pico de gallo (page 128)

1. Preheat a heavy (preferably cast iron) sauté pan over medium heat. Toss the chicken thighs with the oil. Starting with the skin side down, cook the thighs without turning until the skin is very crisp and the fat rendered out. You may gently move the chicken so it does not stick to the pan, but don't turn the pieces over until the skin is very crisp and golden-to-dark brown. Turn and cook until done. If the skin isn't crisp enough, turn and cook skin-side down for several minutes longer. Sprinkle the crisp skin with the salt. (The chicken may also be roasted, skinside up and uncovered, in a 375-degree oven until well-done and golden-crisp, about 35 minutes.)

2. While the chicken is cooking, crush the garlic with a pinch of salt to a smooth paste and stir it into the mayonnaise. Thin the aioli with the extra-virgin olive oil.

3. Thinly slice the chicken, trying to keep some skin on each slice. Place a bit of chicken in a warm tortilla; top it with crumbled bacon, a spoonful of aioli, and jalapeños to taste. Add shredded lettuce and a little pico de gallo.

VARIATION: Add crumbled blue cheese or sharp white cheddar.

JAIBA.
Frita o' al..
Mojo de AJO.

OCKTELES.
amarón - Pulpo
ta de mula - Ostión
mpechanas y Almeja.

BEBIDAS.
CERVEZAS
SODAS.

OOS...!

LEMON-GARLIC CHICKEN TACO
WITH MEZCAL

Makes 12 small tacos. We like to think that marinades impart flavor, but in truth most contribute only moisture and salt, while the fresh tastes of herbs and citrus are lost in the cooking process. The solution? Toss the meat with all those great flavors *after* it's cooked. This sauce is pure spicy-lemon-garlic flavor; it can also be served on the side. Traditional salsas are vegetable-based, but more and more, Mexican cooks are expanding their horizons and creating sauces like this one, a variation on a Caribbean mojo sauce. Thanks to travel, immigration, and the Internet, Latin and South American cuisines are becoming better known in Mexican cities.

4 large boneless chicken thighs, with skin on

1 teaspoon olive oil

Kosher salt

1 large clove garlic, peeled and finely minced

1 small serrano chile, minced

Fresh-ground black pepper

½ lemon

½ lime

1½ teaspoons mezcal or blanco tequila

2 tablespoons chopped cilantro

12 (4-inch) corn tortillas, warmed

Shredded lettuce

1 avocado, diced, sprinkled with a little salt

1. Preheat a cast-iron sauté pan over medium heat. Toss the chicken thighs with the oil. Starting with the skin side down, cook the thighs until the skin is very crisp. Turn and cook them until done. Sprinkle the crisp skin with a little salt. (The chicken may also be roasted, skin side up and uncovered, in a 375-degree oven until well-done and golden-crisp.)

2. When the chicken is cooked, slice it thinly or dice it. Place it in a bowl and toss it with the garlic and serrano chile, ½ teaspoon salt, and a couple grinds of fresh pepper. Squeeze the lime and lemon juice directly over the chicken, add the mezcal, and stir in the cilantro. Serve wrapped in the warm tortillas with lettuce and avocado.

CHIPOTLE DUCK TACO
WITH DUCK CHICHARRÓN,
PINEAPPLE CUCUMBER SALSA, AND SPICY CREMA

Makes 12 large tacos. Duck? Belgian endive? This sophisticated taco is an example of the kind of innovative cooking stirring things up in Mexico City. The upper tier of modern chefs in Mexico (as the city is called) generally have classical kitchen training, as well as experience working in Europe and, often, in Asia. They turn tradition on its head, mixing up preparations, adding Mexican flavors to other cuisines (and vice versa), incorporating new ingredients and rediscovering old ones, and generally having lots of fun. There are several steps to creating this *nuevo* taco, but everything up to the final steps may be done well ahead of time, and at the last minute you need only do the final duck cooking. Just before serving, warm the tortillas and assemble the tacos.

2 (12-ounce) duck breasts	1 teaspoon kosher salt
2½ tablespoons olive oil (divided use)	1 teaspoon white sugar
1 teaspoon ground dried chipotles	Spicy crema (recipe follows)
1 teaspoon ground California or guajillo chiles	Pineapple cucumber salsa (page 137)
1 teaspoon paprika	Shredded red and white Belgian endive (or Savoy cabbage)
1 teaspoon dried Mexican oregano, rubbed to a powder	Lime wedges
	12 warm corn tortillas

1. Remove the skin from the duck breasts. Cut the skin into thin strips and set it aside.

2. Heat a heavy sauté pan over medium heat. Add 1 teaspoon of the oil and sear the duck breasts for 3 minutes per side. Remove them from the pan—the duck will still be rare. At this point, you can refrigerate the duck for up to 24 hours.

3. Preheat the oven to 325 degrees. Arrange the duck skin pieces in a single layer on a rimmed cookie sheet lightly coated with about ½ teaspoon oil and bake for 20 to 30 minutes, or until the skin is browned and very crisp. Remove the strips from pan while hot, salt lightly, and drain them on paper towels. At this point you may store the duck chicharrón for 24 hours; re-crisp them in a 400-degree oven before using.

4. Prepare the chipotle rub by combining the dried chiles, paprika, oregano, salt, and sugar in a small bowl (see note).

5. Half an hour before serving, thinly slice the duck. Toss the duck meat with 1 tablespoon of the olive oil and 2 or 3 tablespoons chipotle rub, enough to coat the meat lightly but evenly.

6. Five minutes before serving, heat a heavy pan over medium-high heat. Add 1 tablespoon of the oil. When the pan is hot, but not smoking, add the duck meat all at once and cook it quickly, stirring often, until the meat is barely pink. Serve right away with the duck skin chicharrón, spicy crema, salsa, endive, limes, and tortillas, and allow guests to assemble their own tacos.

NOTE: The chipotle rub used in this recipe is delicious on grilled meats, fish, or vegetables. Consider making a double or triple recipe so you will have some left over.

SPICY CREMA

Makes 1½ cups.

1 cup sour cream or Mexican crema agria

Zest and juice of ½ orange

½ teaspoon salt

¼ cup (5 or 6 pieces) finely chopped chipotles in adobo

Combine all the ingredients, and taste for seasoning.

MUSHROOM, RAJAS, AND CORN TACO
WITH QUESO FRESCO

Makes 6 large tacos. The earliest Mexican cuisine was vegetable-based, so in times past, before Spanish beef, chicken, and pork worked their way into every taco, there were no doubt plenty of satisfying vegetable taco recipes. Today most vegetables are consumed as salsas, in soups, or stuffed into quesadillas and empanadas, but there's no reason why a vegetable taco shouldn't be every bit as tasty and unusual as any other. This sumptuous vegetarian feast is based on the classic combination of roasted poblano chiles and mushrooms, with the addition of corn and mild-flavored, soft queso fresco. This taco is often favored by even the most committed carnivores. In other seasons, bits of diced cooked sweet potato, zucchini, chayote, squash blossoms, or golden winter squash would be welcome additions.

Fresh epazote, used as a flavoring in this taco, has a minty-oregano taste and is often available at Mexican markets. (It is also hardy and easy to grow.) Fresh or dried mint or Mexican oregano may be substituted, but do not substitute dried epazote.

2 Anaheim chiles

1 poblano chile

1 cup fresh corn kernels (about 1 ear)

1½ tablespoons olive oil

Kosher salt

½ white onion, peeled and cut into ½-inch dice

1 large clove garlic, thinly sliced

6 ounces cremini or white button mushrooms, trimmed and quartered

6 fresh epazote leaves, chopped (about 1 tablespoon, optional)

Fresh-ground black pepper

½ cup queso fresco, cut into small cubes

6 warm corn tortillas

Salsa quemada (page 129)

¼ cup grated cotixa or añejo cheese

Cilantro sprigs

1. Roast the chiles as for rajas (page 92) and cut them into ½-inch dice.

2. Heat a heavy pan (preferably cast iron) over medium-high heat until very hot.

3. In a bowl, toss the corn with 1 teaspoon of the olive oil and a sprinkling of salt. Spread the corn in the hot pan and let it blacken slightly, without stirring, for 30 seconds. Have a lid ready in case the kernels begin to pop. Remove the roasted corn from the pan.

4. In the same pan, heat 2 teaspoons of the olive oil. Add the onion and diced chiles and cook, stirring often, until the onion is soft and beginning to brown. Season lightly with salt and remove from the pan.

5. Reduce the heat and add the remaining olive oil. Add the garlic and mushrooms. Cook, stirring often, until the mushrooms are cooked through, 2 to 3 minutes. Return the corn and chiles to the pan and stir to reheat.

6. Turn off the heat and stir in the epazote, if using, black pepper, and queso fresco.

7. To assemble the tacos, spoon some vegetables onto a tortilla. Top with a generous tablespoon of salsa and sprinkle about 1 teaspoon of cotixa cheese over all. Top with a cilantro sprig.

MORE VEGETARIAN TACO FILLINGS

✤ Cooked pinto beans, queso fresco, cilantro, and pico de gallo.

✤ Grilled corn, beans, pico de gallo, melted cheese, scallions, and pickled jalapeños prepared as a taco *dorado* (page 114).

✤ Onions sautéed with diced zucchini and corn with ripe red chiles.

✤ Roasted, skinned and seeded poblano chiles sautéed with slivers of garlic and onions, finished with a spoonful of thick sour cream

✤ Cubed and roasted squash, black beans, spicy pico de gallo and cotixa cheese

CHILE RELLENO TACO
WITH SALSA QUEMADA

Makes 6 hefty tacos. I see chile relleno tacos occasionally in the smaller Mexican *fondas* (small, sit-down restaurants): it's not a street item. This makes for a hefty taco—as well as a goopy, saucy and rich one, which must be double-wrapped. A single taco is usually enough for most people for a meal. Poblano chiles are used to make chiles rellenos in Mexico, but be aware that they have a tendency to be unexpectedly spicy. Long, pale-green Anaheim chiles are always mild and tasty.

Salsa quemada (page 129)

6 Anaheim or small poblano chiles

3 ounces Jack cheese, cut into 6 fingers

1 large egg

½ cup flour

2 tablespoons vegetable oil

12 warm corn tortillas

½ cup grated cotixa cheese

Cilantro sprigs

1. Make the salsa quemada and keep warm.

2. Char and prepare the chiles as for rajas (page 92), leaving the stems on. Cut a small slit up one side of each chile and carefully remove all seeds, using a small teaspoon. Insert a piece of cheese into each chile and fold the chile so that it completely encloses the cheese.

3. Separate the egg. Beat the yolk to loosen it. Beat the white until fluffy, then gently fold in the yolk. Put the mixture in a shallow bowl. Pour the flour into a saucer and add the salt.

4. Heat the oil in a 10-inch sauté pan and when it is hot, dip each chile into the egg, allow the excess to drip off, and roll it in the flour. Shake off excess flour and fry the chiles on both sides until they golden brown and the cheese inside is melted.

5. To assemble the tacos, wrap each chile in 2 warm corn tortillas, top with salsa quemada and a sprinkle on a bit of cotixa cheese. Top with a cilantro sprig. Enjoy very hot.

VARIATION: Stuff the tacos with goat cheese rather than Jack cheese, or with sautéed fresh corn and onions.

CHAPTER 4

SALSAS AND BASICS

A Dios rogando y con el mazo dando.

(Pray to God and swing a hammer.)

The immediacy of a taco, handed to you hot from grill and comal, can't be equaled. You can stand there and eat yourself silly with one taco after another, each made fresh for you and consumed within seconds. A *great* taco rocks with distinct tastes that roll on and on, like a little party on your tongue, with layers of flavor and textures: juicy, delicious fillings, perfectly seasoned; the taste of the soft corn tortilla; a morsel of salty cheese and finally, best of all, the bright explosion of a freshly-made salsa that suddenly ignites and unites everything on your palate. At the end of your two- or three-bite taco you just want to repeat the experience until you are sated.

That essential salsa is far more than just a sauce. It completes the taco the way icing completes a cake. It's about balance again, as you add not only flavor but color and texture as well, carefully chosen to complement the filling. Rich and meaty tacos need an acidic salsa, such as one made with tomatillos and coarse salt. Citrus flavors such as lemon and lime jump out with a the touch of hot salsa. Fresh tomato, onion and cilantro go with almost anything, especially a creamy melted cheese, or a smoky char-roasted chile. Fish and shrimp fairly pop with fresh hot peppers and fruit, given an herbal edge with cilantro. Throwing on just any salsa, or too many different salsas, misses the point completely.

Choose impeccable ingredients of great character—ripe tomatoes, fragrant mangoes, fierce chilies, vibrant cilantro, and lime. Be bold and unafraid! Go a little over the top with your seasoning. Timidity has no place in a salsa. Remember, each taco will have only a small amount of salsa, and the salsa has to stand up to all the other tastes and unite them. The flavor of acid, salt, sweetness, and heat escalate when the salsa is properly, that is to say, assertively seasoned. A perfectly crafted salsa will seem almost too powerful, but each taste will balance the others, and that little taste will make your simple taco exceptional.

PICO DE GALLO
(FRESH TOMATO SALSA)

Makes 2½ cups. The simplest salsa of all—ripe tomatoes, seeded and diced, mixed with sweet onions, cilantro, lime, a pinch of salt, and fresh hot chiles. If you prefer, omit the hot chiles; then you have salsa fresca. For a more picante salsa, increase the chiles. Good tomatoes are a must for this salsa, which is a classic, served on all types of tacos. I prefer to use roma or plum-type tomatoes that are ripe but firm. When tomatoes are out of season, or not great, try making salsa quemada with them instead (recipe follows).

4 large, ripe Roma tomatoes, cored, seeded, and diced small (about 2 cups)

½ cup finely diced white onion

½ medium serrano chile, minced

½ cup loosely packed, roughly chopped cilantro leaves

½ teaspoon salt, or to taste

1 tablespoon fresh lime juice, or to taste

Combine all the ingredients 1 hour before serving. Taste for seasoning and add more salt or lime juice as needed. This salsa is good for 24 hours, refrigerated, but may need to be drained and reseasoned.

SALSA QUEMADA
(ROASTED TOMATO SALSA)

Makes 2½ cups. A very useful salsa that is easy to make and keeps well. Firm, fresh Roma tomatoes are dry-roasted until soft and well charred on all sides (*quemada* literally means "burnt"), then pureed into a smooth salsa with sweet toasted garlic, fresh cilantro, and onion. Salsa quemada clings to the dryer and chunkier taco fillings, adding moisture and great flavor. It is also a classic table salsa, perfect to serve with tostadas and totopos.

5 large Roma tomatoes, whole, not cored or cut in any way

1 serrano or jalapeño chile

2 cloves garlic, skin on

¼ cup minced white onion

1 teaspoon salt, or to taste

½ bunch cilantro

1. Make sure your kitchen is well ventilated. Put a piece of aluminum foil in a heavy sauté pan (preferably cast iron) and set it over medium-high heat. Place the whole tomatoes, chile, and garlic cloves in the pan and dry-roast them on all sides until well charred and soft. The garlic and chiles will be done quickly; the tomatoes may take 10 minutes or longer to cook.

2. Peel the garlic and stem the chile. Place the tomatoes, garlic, and chile in a food processor with the onion, salt, and cilantro. Pulse until the salsa is smooth and taste for seasoning. The salsa will keep, refrigerated, for several days. Reseason before use.

MAYONESA SAUCE
FOR FISH TACOS

Makes about ½ cup. This is the legendary "secret sauce," a fixture at fish taco stands, where you add it yourself from a pump dispenser. Use small amounts to enhance any seafood taco—or a *perro caliente*.

- ½ cup mayonnaise
- ¼ teaspoon kosher salt
- 1 tablespoon fresh-squeezed lime juice
- 1 tablespoon finely chopped cilantro

Whisk all ingredients together. The mayonesa keeps, refrigerated, for 48 hours.

AVOCADO CILANTRO SAUCE

Makes about ¾ cup. A taco stand staple, this simple sauce adds flavor and helps to stick your taco together.

- ½ avocado
- ¼ teaspoon salt, or to taste
- Juice of ½ lime, or to taste
- 1–2 tablespoons water
- 1 tablespoon chopped cilantro

Combine all the ingredients in a blender, using the smaller amount of water. Puree until smooth and add more water, if needed, to make an easily spreadable consistency. Taste for salt and lime, but do not overseason; this sauce should be on the bland side. It keeps, refrigerated, for 24 hours.

SALSA DE CHILES DE ARBOL
(HOT SAUCE)

Makes 2 cups. It's fine for taco fillings to have a little spicy zip—chiles bring out flavor in much the same way as salt and lime—but *serious* heat should only be added judiciously by the individual diner in the form of a good hot salsa, so that everyone may adjust the taco to taste. This particular sauce, made from dagger-shaped chiles de arbol, has an enjoyable sharp heat that quickly dissipates. (In fact, the salsa itself will not be as hot after an hour or so.) It is excellent on anything rich or cheesy.

- 2 Roma tomatoes
- 3 large garlic cloves, skin on
- 1 teaspoon olive oil
- 1 cup stemmed and seeded chiles de arbol
- 1 cup water
- 1 teaspoon white vinegar, or to taste
- ½ teaspoon kosher salt, or to taste

1. Make sure your kitchen is well ventilated. Lay a sheet of aluminum foil in a heavy sauté pan (preferably cast iron) over medium-high heat. Set the whole tomatoes and garlic cloves on the foil and roast until blackened in several places, turning them only infrequently. Peel the garlic and place it, along with the tomatoes, in a blender jar.

2. Add the olive oil and chiles de arbol to the same pan and cook, stirring, until the chiles start to blacken. Remove the pan from the heat and pour in the water. Soak the chiles for 30 minutes. Add this mixture to the blender.

3. Puree the salsa for several minutes, until smooth. Add vinegar and salt to taste. If the salsa is bitter, try adding a pinch more salt. The salsa keeps, refrigerated, for up to 7 days.

VARIATION: To make the salsa (significantly) hotter, roast one or two whole habaneros alongside the garlic until soft. Remove the stems and puree, seeds and all, with the salsa.

SALSA BORRACHA
(DRIED CHILE SALSA WITH TEQUILA)

Makes 2 cups. *Borracho* means "drunk" and there is an entire family of borracho foods. Very little alcohol is used in any of them, with the possible exception of refried beans with beer, which uses a whole bottle. Borracha (tipsy) salsas are spiked with a light touch of beer, tequila, or *pulque* (another fermented agave product), but they are never strong or overwhelming. This recipe is made of two kinds of dried chiles, which must be cooked to bring out their bright berry and tobacco flavors. The salsa is brilliant with lamb and beef, very good with eggs, and terrific as an enchilada sauce.

2 dried pasilla or ancho chiles

2 dried California or guajillo chiles

1 dried chile de arbol

½ cup water

3 Roma tomatoes

2 large cloves of garlic, skin on

¼ cup minced white onion

1 bunch cilantro

2 teaspoons kosher salt, or to taste

1 tablespoon blanco tequila

1. Heat a heavy pan (preferably cast iron) over medium-high heat. Toast the chiles quickly on both sides until fragrant, but do not allow them to burn. Cool them, remove the stems and seeds, and tear them into small pieces. Place the chiles in a small pan with the water and bring to a boil. Turn off heat and soak the chiles for 30 minutes, or until soft.

2. While the chiles soak, set a piece of aluminum foil in the same heavy pan and place it over medium-high heat. Roast the whole tomatoes and garlic cloves until soft and well charred on all sides. Peel the garlic.

3. In a blender, puree the chiles with the soaking liquid. Add the tomatoes, peeled garlic, onion, cilantro ,and salt. Pulse until the salsa is smooth.

4. Stir in the tequila and taste for salt. The salsa will keep, refrigerated, for up to 1 week.

RAW TOMATILLO SALSA

Makes 1 cup. Tomatillos look like small green tomatoes in sticky, papery husks. In fact, they are relatives of the tomato and are a type of ground cherry. They are native to Central America. Fresh-tasting and excitingly tart, this chunky salsa is great on grilled meat, tostadas, or seafood. It can be made in less than a minute and should be used immediately.

4 large tomatillos, papery husks removed

2 tablespoons diced white onion

1 serrano chile, stemmed

8 sprigs cilantro, stemmed

½ teaspoon salt, or to taste

1. Wash the tomatillos well with warm water to remove the naturally sticky coating, which is bitter. Cut them into quarters.

2. Pulse the tomatillos in a food processor with the remaining ingredients until a slightly chunky texture is achieved.

3. Taste for salt and serve as soon as possible to enjoy maximum bite and crunch.

ROASTED TOMATILLO SALSA

Makes 2½ cups. This salsa, made with lightly roasted tomatillos and tomatoes, is less acidic than the raw version. It perfectly balances rich-tasting foods like lengua, carne asada, pork, duck, shrimp and lobster, and cheeses. It is also delicious as a table salsa with tostadas. To make it spicier, use a second jalapeño.

- 6 large tomatillos, papery husks removed
- 2 Roma tomatoes
- 1 large jalapeño chile
- 2 large garlic cloves, skin on
- ½ teaspoon salt, or to taste
- ½ cup chopped cilantro (optional)

1. Make sure your kitchen is well ventilated. Place a sheet of aluminum foil in a large, heavy frying pan (preferably cast iron). Set the pan over medium-high heat.

2. Wash and dry the tomatillos, tomatoes, and jalapeño. Roast them whole, along with the garlic cloves, until charred on all sides, turning them several times. Stem the jalapeño and peel the garlic. Place all the roasted items in a blender jar and pulse until pureed. Add the salt and stir in the chopped cilantro, if desired. Taste again for seasoning just before serving—sometimes a pinch more salt is called for.

SALSA VERDE
(AVOCADO TOMATILLO SALSA)

Makes 1½ cups. Pale green and lovely, with a nice tartness balanced by creamy avocado, this is winner on everything. It may be used in place of avocado cilantro sauce on tacos, or as a quick alternative to roasted tomatillo salsa.

1 ripe Hass avocado, peeled and pitted

3 large tomatillos, husked and well washed

½ serrano chile

1 large clove garlic, peeled

2 tablespoons minced white onion

1½ teaspoons salt

½ bunch cilantro, chopped

In a food processor combine the avocado, tomatillos, chile, garlic, onion, and salt. Pulse until the sauce is pureed. Add the chopped cilantro and pulse several more times. The salsa will keep, refrigerated, for 24 hours. Reseason before use.

MANGO
HABANERO SALSA

Makes 1½ cups. Fruit of all kinds is widely used in Mexican cooking, in everything from mole sauces to drinks to guacamoles to, of course, salsas. Mango salsa is probably the best known. Though many recipes exist, the goal is to create a wonderful combination of tartness, heat, and sweet fruit. Mango salsa has a special affinity for shrimp, lobster, and chicken. In season, Asian and Mexican markets carry small, luscious Manila mangoes, which are ideal for this salsa when they are ripe but still firm. Habanero chile is very spicy—that's part of the fun—but you can substitute a milder chile, or leave it out altogether, if you prefer.

- ¾ cup firm but ripe mango, peeled and cut into ⅜-inch dice
- ½ cup roma tomato, cored and cut into small dice
- 2 tablespoons finely diced red onion
- ½ teaspoon minced habanero chile
- 1 tablespoon fresh-squeezed lime juice, or to taste
- ¼ teaspoon kosher salt, or to taste
- ½ teaspoon sugar
- ½ teaspoon rice vinegar
- ½ teaspoon chopped fresh mint leaves
- 1 tablespoon chopped cilantro

Combine all the ingredients. Taste for seasoning; the salsa should be full-flavored, both sweet and very hot. You may need to add more lime juice or salt. This salsa should be used within 2 hours.

PINEAPPLE CUCUMBER SALSA

Makes 2½ cups. Pineapple is native to South America and was known and used by the ancient Mexicans. It is widely grown in Mexico and is one of the most popular fruits in a fruit-loving nation. This crunchy salsa has a wonderful scent and many uses. It's great on anything grilled, served with tostadas as an antojito, stirred into ceviche, or as the base for a cold seafood salad. Make sure it has a powerful lime punch, and don't be afraid of the salt; that brings up the sweetness of the fruit.

1 cup finely diced ripe pineapple

½ cup finely diced jicama

¼ cup finely diced cucumber

¼ cup finely diced red bell pepper

1 tablespoon finely diced red onion

1 tablespoon fresh-squeezed lime juice, or to taste

1 teaspoon rice vinegar

¼ teaspoon salt, or to taste

2 tablespoons chopped cilantro

Combine the ingredients 1 hour before serving. Stir and taste, correct seasoning, especially the lime or salt, if needed. Use this salsa the same day it is made.

CHIPOTLE SALSA

Makes about ½ cup. Mayonesa-based salsas of all kinds have become increasingly popular at taco stands, adding richness and creamy flavor to otherwise simple tacos. The most common is the lime-sparkled mayonesa so essential to the taste of the real fish taco. You will find many uses for this smoky chipotle version. Chipotles are ripe jalapeños that have been slowly dried over wood smoke. They may be purchased whole, ground, or canned in adobo—that is, reconstituted with tomato sauce, vinegar, and a touch of sweetness. Try this salsa on crisp oven-roasted potatoes or on a chicken sandwich; you will find many other uses for it as well.

- ½ cup mayonnaise
- 2 tablespoons finely chopped chipotles in adobo
- 1 teaspoon fresh-squeezed lime juice, or to taste
- 1 teaspoon water (optional, see note)

Stir together all the ingredients in a small bowl. The sauce keeps, refrigerated, for up to 1 week.

NOTE: If you plan to serve the sauce from a squeeze bottle, which can be convenient, puree the sauce in a blender and add 1 teaspoon water to thin it.

VARIATION: Add 1 or 2 cloves fresh peeled garlic, finely minced. Refrigerate until needed.

CHILE LIME SAUCE

Makes ¾ cup. Asian ingredients such as fiery sambal paste and Chinese chile paste are widely used in the United States and have made inroads into new Mexican cooking too, possibly as a convenience item—a kick in a jar, if you will. This creamy salsa is good with anything fried or cheesy. It must be very spicy or the effect is lost, but the sweetness of the citrus is a perfect counterpoint.

½ cup mayonnaise

3½ tablespoons sambal or red chili paste

1 tablespoon fresh-squeezed lime juice

Zest of 1 orange or lemon

Combine all ingredients. The sauce keeps, refrigerated, for 48 hours.

THE COMAL

The *comal* is a simple griddle and the busiest piece of equipment in the Mexican kitchen. Cooks set this disk of thin steel or earthenware directly over a flame to cook tortillas, toast chiles and nuts, or char vegetables for salsa. I find it best to use cheap, well-seasoned cast-iron pans. Don't use nonstick pans; the high heat required to properly toast ingredients can vaporize the coating, producing unhealthy fumes.

The toasting and dry-roasting of ingredients are important techniques to master, especially when making salsa. *Toasting* involves cooking in a hot, dry pan, stirring all the while, until the ingredient is fragrant but never burned. *Dry-roasting* is the process used to char and blacken fresh vegetables.

TIP: Line the pan with a piece of aluminum foil to prevent sticking. Always make sure there is plenty of ventilation when you cook with this sort of high heat, and especially when you roast chiles.

BLACK BEANS
WITH EPAZOTE

Makes 3 cups. Black beans are most often associated with the cooking of southern Mexico and the Yucatán. The beans are usually cooked with a sprig of epazote, a wild herb; it has a mildly minty/herbal taste and is thought to aid the digestion.

1 cup dried black beans, washed and picked over

8–10 cups water

1 sprig fresh epazote

2 cloves garlic, peeled

1 whole white onion, peeled, plus 2 tablespoons minced white onion

1 serrano chile, washed

2 teaspoons kosher salt, or to taste

1 teaspoon lard or olive oil

¼ teaspoon crushed red chiles

1. Combine the beans, water, epazote, 1 garlic clove, the whole peeled onion, and the serrano chile in a 4-quart saucepan. Bring the mixture to a steady simmer over medium heat and cook uncovered for 1 hour.

2. Add the salt and continue simmering for 3 hours longer, or until the beans are very tender. Make sure there is always enough water in the pot that the beans move easily. Add more water as needed.

3. When the beans are done, fish out the onion, garlic, chile, and epazote, and discard them. Cool the beans in the cooking liquid. Mince the remaining garlic clove and set it aside.

4. Just before serving, heat the lard in a sauté pan. Add the minced onion and cook until soft; add the minced garlic and red chile and cook 1 minute longer.

5. Taste for seasoning and add more salt if necessary.

VARIATION: Instead of serving the beans whole, mash them in the sauté pan, ladleful by ladleful. Add plenty of the cooking liquid as you mash the beans—if necessary, add extra water (or a little beer). You want them to be mostly smooth, but some texture is desirable. The ideal refritos are softer and creamier than mashed potatoes.

SOURCES

With the exception of a few ingredients, such as certain dried chiles or masa harina, the ingredients for these recipes are easily found in any produce shop or supermarket. Even the less common items are easy to find online or in specialty markets.

MARKETS Most large cities now have Mexican or Latin markets, from small neighborhood shops to large supermarkets. In Southern California, the Northgate González and El Metate chains offer every kind of fresh, canned, and dried ingredient, as well as full meat and fish counters, Mexican delis, and *tortillerias*. On the East Coast, Caribbean and Latin markets often carry Mexican products, or they may be able to direct you to a Mexican market.

ONLINE SOURCES

The Specialty Cheese Company Visit specialcheese.com or call 1-800-367-1711, extension 22. All kinds of cheeses from all around the world.

Woodlandfoods Visit woodlandfoods.com or call 847-625-8600. A good source for dried chiles, dried corn, masa harina.

Mexgrocer.com Visit the website or call 877-463-9476. A source for tools as well as ingredients.

Latinmerchant.com Visit the website or call 206-223-9374. A wide selection of dried and canned Mexican and Caribbean ingredients.

MiFiesta.com Visit the website or call 770-454-0550. Candies, Mexican foods, tamales, tools, and cookware.

RECOMMENDED READING To learn basic techniques such as making tortillas, and for a thorough grounding in traditional Mexican cooking, I recommend any of Diana Kennedy's excellent books, but especially *The Art of Mexican Cooking* (Clarkson Potter, 2008) and *The Cuisines of Mexico* (William Morrow, 1989). The books are well-illustrated and well-written, and they don't stray from traditional preparations. I like *Seasons of My Heart* (Ballantine, 1999), by Susana Trilling, on traditional Oaxacan regional cooking. If you read Spanish (or are very patient and have a good English-Spanish dictionary), *Larousse de la Cocina Mexicana* (Larousse, 2007), by Alicia Gironella and Giorgio de'Angeli, is an outstanding reference book.

CHILES

FRESH If possible, purchase your fresh chiles at a Mexican market. Fresh chiles should be firm and unwrinkled. Disposable gloves should be worn when handling any fresh chile. Avoid touching eyes or skin, and wash the cutting board and knife as soon as you are finished with them. Since the heat in chiles resides in the seeds and ribs, you may adjust the heat of any recipe by seeding the chiles, or increase it by leaving the seeds in.

Anaheim or California Mild to medium heat. Long, narrow and light green. These chiles are best cooked and are good to stuff for chiles rellenos or to char and tear into strips for rajas.

Bell pepper Sweet. The familiar round green, yellow, orange, or red pepper. Use them raw or roasted in soups, salads, and rice; many recipes call for stuffing them.

Güero Mild to medium heat. Smaller, yellow to pale green, rounded tip, hollow. Best cooked, and good for stuffing or grilling.

Habanero Very, *very* hot. Small round red, orange, or yellow chiles, with pronounced ribbing. These chiles are usually used raw, but may be roasted. Use with care only when lots of heat is desired.

Jalapeño Medium heat. Smaller and wider at the stem than the serrano, pointed, green to dark green. Best raw or roasted for salsas, pickling, grilling, and stuffing.

Poblano Mild to medium heat. Large, shiny, dark green to almost black, wide at the stem and sharply pointed. Char and use them for rajas; stuff them as chiles rellenos; use them roasted and diced in fillings, soups, sauces and salsas; puree them and add them to rice.

Serrano Medium to hot. Small, narrow, green, and very firm. Use them raw or roasted for salsas.

Red Fresno Sweet to mild. Shaped like jalapeños and about the same size, but come in red, yellow, and orange. Use raw or roasted, for stuffing and grilling.

DRIED Dried chiles have very specific tastes and uses. The chiles below are the most commonly used in Mexican cooking. At the store, look for dried chiles that are leathery and flexible, never brittle. There should be no sign of dust or bug infestation. Dried chiles keep indefinitely frozen inside doubled freezer bags. To prepare them for cooking, remove the stem and (usually) the seeds from large chiles. The seeds are sometimes used in moles and may also be left in hot chiles, to increase the heat. Dry chiles must always be cooked, either by being toasted or sautéed, then soaked and pureed, or by being soaked, pureed, and fried.

Chile de arbol Hot. Long, thin, bright red, with lots of seeds that can be left in for more heat.

Guajillo Usually mild, but a picante type is sometimes sold (and is always labeled as such). Burgundy, nearly black, smooth skinned, shiny. One of the most widely used chiles for salsas and moles.

Ancho Mild to medium heat. Made by drying the poblano chile, this type looks like a giant raisin, with dark brown to black, wrinkled skin. Good for salsas, spice rubs, and moles.

Chipotle Hot and smoky. Made from ripe jalapeños that have been dried over wood smoke. Available whole, ground, or canned in adobo. Best for salsas and marinades.

ESSENTIAL INGREDIENTS
AND SUBSTITUTIONS

Avocado Choose Hass avocados, which have a dark, pebbly skin. The avocado should yield when gently pressed.

Chiles see sidebar.

Cilantro Wash it in the bunch, shake off the excess water, and store it in the refrigerator with the stems in a glass of water, loosely covered with a plastic bag.

Garlic Buy whole heads of firm garlic. Break off cloves and peel them as needed. For dry-roasted garlic, roast the cloves with the skin on in a dry pan lined with aluminum foil, turning them several times, until soft.

Limes Fresh-squeezed lime juice is essential for best flavor. When buying limes, choose small ones with thin, smooth skins (but not tiny Key limes). Yellow patches on the skin indicate ripeness and are not necessarily a flaw.

Onion Use white or red onions, which have a mild, sweet taste. If you want to tone down the bite of raw onion, rinse with cold water after dicing and dry.

Salt Use kosher salt, which is evenly coarse and has no additives. (Table salt contains iodine, which can be bitter, as well as anticlumping additives.) If you use sea salt, start with half the amount called for and adjust to taste.

Tomato All recipes in the book are designed to be made with ripe Roma or plum-type tomatoes, which have great taste and contain less water and fewer seeds than beefsteak-type tomatoes. If tomatoes are out of season consider making salsa quemada (page 129) or another type, such as salsa verde, instead of pico de gallo.

Tortillas The flavor of the corn tortilla is an essential part of the taste of the tacos in this book. On the street, tacos are *always* made with warm corn tortillas. If you do not have access to fresh tortillas, most supermarkets carry decent corn tortillas, or try making your own from Maseca masa harina.

GLOSSARY

Achiote Spice paste (*recado*) originating in the Yucatán, made of annatto seeds, citrus, vinegar, and garlic. Used on roast pork (*cocinita pibil*) and fish.

Adobo Marinade or wet seasoning rub for meat or fish; also, the sauce canned chipotles are packed in.

Agave nectar Agave juice boiled down to make a sweet syrup. Simple syrup or honey may be substituted in many cases.

Agua fresca A popular drink made of mashed fresh fruit and water, lime juice, and a little sugar. Favorite flavors for agua fresca include watermelon, jamaica (hibiscus), tamarind, lemon-lime, pineapple, and guava.

Aguachiles Raw shellfish (usually shrimp or scallops) mixed, at the moment of service, with lime juice, sliced cucumber, and onion, and sprinkled with ground hot chiles. May also be made with pureed hot chiles and lime juice.

Al gusto Literally "to taste" but, more specifically, to *your* taste. At a taco stand, for example, you are expected to finish your taco *al gusto* with provided salsas, garnishes, lime, and salt.

Al pastor Spice-rubbed pork cooked on a upright spit.

Allspice A dried berry (*Pimenta dioica*) native to Mexico and the Caribbean, which has mild overtones of cinnamon, nutmeg, and clove. Called *pimienta de Jamaica* in Mexico.

Amor Love, passion

Añejo Old or aged

Antojito A snack or appetizer; a small plate

Birria Goat meat stewed with dry chiles and tomatoes.

Blender For pureeing salsas and soaked chiles.

Borracho/borracha Drunken, or made with with alcohol.

Botánica Shop that sells dry herbs, candles, incense and religious figurines as well as prayer candles, potions, and icons.

Box grater For grating cheeses and vegetables such as carrots.

Braise To cook slowly with a small amount of liquid until tender (usually meat).

Cactus Many types of cactus are consumed in Mexico. The most common, nopal, is the paddle of the beavertail cactus. After being dethorned, cut up, and boiled, it is added to salsas or scrambled with eggs. Cactus fruit, such as the tuna (also called cactus apple) and pithaya (also known as dragon fruit), are also consumed, usually raw. Chunks of candied cactus may be purchased in most Mexican markets.

Calabasa, calabacita Squash, both hardshell and summer types

Cantinero Bartender

Capeado Batter-dipped; the itself word means "wrapped, or enfolded."

Carne, carne asada *Carne* means "meat." Carne asada is thin-sliced beef cut from the top round, quickly marinated (usually with lime, garlic, oil, and salt), and grilled over a hot charcoal fire.

Carnitas Pork, slow-cooked until it is very tender and shredded.

Cast-iron pans Well seasoned, various sizes. Note: Nonstick pans should never be used over heat high enough to char tomatoes or roast chiles, as the coating may vaporize.

Ceviche Raw fish or shellfish "cooked" in fresh citrus juice and mixed with vegetables. Originated in South America, but widely appreciated.

Café de olla Strong coffee brewed with cinnamon sticks, other spices, and piloncillo—raw sugar.

Chayote Pale green, pear shaped vegetable (also known as christophene or mirliton) with a taste and texture similar to zucchini. Spiny chayote must be peeled. The leaves are sometimes used in cooking.

Cheeses The most common Mexican cheeses include fresh cheeses such as panela and queso fresco, which are creamy-tasting and rubbery. Jack and Oaxaca are excellent melting cheeses. Cotixa is a dry, salty cheese to be crumbled on top of beans, tacos, and enchiladas.

Chicharrón, chicharrónes Pork skin deep-fried in lard until crisp, golden brown, and chewy.

Chipotle See sidebar (page 143).

Chivo Goat

Chocolate Cacao is native to the ancient Mayan regions, and the process of turning it into chocolate through fermenting, roasting, and grinding was also developed by the Maya people. Mexican chocolate (I prefer the Ibarra brand over all others) is gritty with sugar and spiced with cinnamon, cardamom, and ground almonds.

Chupacabra Literally, "goat sucker." The chupacabra is a yeti-like creature that haunts rural Mexico, allegedly sucking the blood out of farm animals and leaving the bodies behind. It has never been photographed.

Cinnamon Mexicans exclusively use Ceylon cinnamon, which has soft, thin bark and a mild flavor. Cinnamon sticks are used more often than ground, except in baking. Most cinnamon sold in the United States is cassia, which is strong and almost hot.

Citrus juicers, various sizes The Mexican juicer is a hinged device that efficiently squeezes and strains with one press. Get medium and large sizes, to fit limes, lemons, and oranges.

Clamato A bottled mixture of clam juice and tomato juice, wildly popular in Mexico as a labor-saving substitute for the juice of fresh shucked clams in cocktails and micheladas.

Comal A flat disk of earthenware or thin blue steel for cooking tortillas and roasting vegetables. A well-seasoned cast-iron griddle or pan (see below) may be used instead.

Cotixa See Cheeses.

Crema Thick cultured cream similar to sour cream or crème fraîche.

Crema de almendrada Tequila-based liqueur flavored with almonds. Amaretto is an acceptable substitute.

Damiana *Turnera diffusa*, or *Turnera aphrodisiaca* is a wild herb that has been used by the people of Central America for thousands of years as a mood elevator and mild relaxant. Damiana is used to make a liqueur of the same name, which is purported to be a mild aphrodisiac.

Diablito Little devil

Dicho Folk sayings and proverbs, passed down orally. Many *dichos* are simple rhyming couplets.

Disca A Mexican cooking pan that looks like a hubcap with a wide, slanted rim. Used for deep-frying, especially fish tacos.

Dorado Golden brown

Epazote A wild herb (*Dysphania ambrosioides*) native to Mexico and South America that now grows wild throughout North America. The leaves have a strong, unusual taste, reminiscent of mint, oregano, and even licorice, with a gamy undertaste. A sprig of epazote is usually added to black beans, and it is used as a cooking herb.

Fajita *Fajita* means "belt or cinch." The modern dish is thought to have evolved from the cooking of Mexican cowboys, who would grill beef and cut it into thin strips. Perhaps the name refers to the thin strips – or the toughness of the meat.

Flor de calabasa Zucchini flowers or squash blossoms, usually the male blossoms (*machos*) which will not produce fruit. May be stuffed with cheese or vegetables, or added to fillings, especially those with rajas or cheese.

Frutas Fruit

Gobernador Governor

Habanero See Chiles sidebar (page 142).

Hacienda Ranch

Hoja santa Leaves of *Piper auritum* widely used as a flavoring in Mexican cooking, especially pre-Spanish traditional foods. It has a mild licorice or anise flavor.

Horno Oven

Hot sauce Meant to be used in tiny droplets to add zip to tacos and soups. My favorite bottled salsas are Salsa Amor and Salsa Huichol, both hot, but tasty. Cholula is also acceptable. These sauces are thick and orange-red from the chiles, and will cling to the food.

Jamaica Dried hibiscus flowers, which may be steeped to make a tart, delicious tea or agua fresca.

Jicama A large tuber in the shape of a slightly flattened sphere. It has a fibrous brown skin that must be peeled away. The flesh is crisp and juicy, faintly sweet. It is usually eaten raw, traditionally with lime juice and ground chiles.

Jugo Juice

Lard Rendered pork fat. For frying, it should be white, with a mild pork flavor. The delicious, soft, tan pork fat reclaimed from carnitas or frying chicharrón is used for flavoring.

Lechuga Lettuce

Lengua Tongue, usually beef tongue. May be purchased at Mexican and some Asian markets.

Lucas spice A popular seasoning mix sold in shakers and put on everything from candy to salads and fruit, as well as being used to rim drinks such as micheladas (page 49). Lucas is made of ground mild chiles and salt, sometimes with ascorbic acid (for tartness). When it is made with ground hot chiles, it is called picante or pico de gallo spice.

Loca Literally, "crazy" but used to describe anything stuffed orr embellished

Macho Male, and proud of it.

Maggi seasoning Bottled seasoning mix along the lines of Worcestershire sauce, used to add a distinctive, salty flavor and a bit of color to soups, sauces, and drinks.

Masa Dough made of ground corn.

Masa harina Instant masa flour, just add water to make tortilla masa. Maseca brand is the best. Make sure it says "for tortillas" on the package; the masa harina made for tamales is coarser.

Mayonesa Mayonnaise. In Mexico, very light and often flavored with lime.

Mojo A Caribbean sauce made of garlic and citrus juice.

Molcajete A lava rock bowl resting on three stubby legs, most often used for making and serving guacamole, but also useful for grinding roasted tomatoes into salsa or for coarsely grinding spices.

Nortena Mexican music with a pulsing, bouncy beat

Oaxaca cheese See Cheeses.

Olla A cooking pot made of terra-cotta, often brightly painted.

Palapa An open-sided hut roofed with palm leaves.

Papas Potatoes

Pepitas Green pumpkin or squash seeds

Perro caliente Mexican hot dog

Piloncillo Raw cane sugar with a molasses flavor, formed into cones.

Plancha Large, flat cooking surface

Plata Silver

Quemada Burned, charred, or caramelized

Rajas Fresh poblano chiles that have been charred, peeled, seeded, and torn into strips

Reposado Literally, "rested." Refers to a tequila that has been barrel-aged after distilling.

Rico Rich or delicious

Sandia Watermelon

Sangria Wine punch, originally Spanish

Sangrita Palate-cleansing drink served alongside tequila or mezcal. Typically made of tomato juice flavored with fresh citrus juices.

Sinaloa Mexican state across the Gulf of California from Baja California Sur, and south of Sonora. Sinaloa has a long, beautiful coastline and many beaches. It is renowned for its seafood cooking.

Spice grinder An electric coffee-type grinder, used only for this purpose, is best for grinding chiles and spices. See also *Molcajete*, below.

Star anise A spice with a large, hard, star-shaped pod. Like anise, it has a strong licorice flavor.

Sustainable Ecologically and economically viable. In reference to fish, the term refers to methods of harvesting that aim to prevent overfishing and the killing of other species as by-catch, as well as choosing fish from large, healthy populations that can support a fishing industry at commercial levels.

Taqueria Taco stand

Taquero / taquera Taco seller

Tomatillo A type of ground cherry that looks like a small, green tomato with a papery husk and is both crunchy and tart.

Torito A small chile, such as a jalapeño or güero, stuffed with various fillings.

Tortillas See Essentials (page 143)

Tostadas, totopos Corn tortillas, fried crisp (page 85), usually served with a dip or topped with something substantial such as mashed beans or salpicón. A less-traditional, but more health-conscious, way to prepare tostadas is to bake them (page 85).

Tripa Tripe

Turista Tourist or foreign visitor

Vampiro / Vampira Vampire

Vaquero Mexican cowboy

Vaso Glass

Verde Green

Viznaga Type of cactus, commonly used for making candied cactus.

Zarandeado A word with many slang meanings, one of which is "shaken or turned."

CONVERSION CHART

Weight Equivalents: The metric weights given in this chart are not exact equivalents, but have been rounded up or down slightly to make measuring easier.

Volume Equivalents: These are not exact equivalents for American cups and spoons, but have been rounded up or down slightly to make measuring easier.

AVOIRDUPOIS	METRIC
¼ oz	7 g
½ oz	15 g
1 oz	30 g
2 oz	60 g
3 oz	90 g
4 oz	115 g
5 oz	150 g
6 oz	175 g
7 oz	200 g
8 oz (½ lb)	225 g
9 oz	250 g
10 oz	300 g
11 oz	325 g
12 oz	350 g
13 oz	375 g
14 oz	400 g
15 oz	425 g
16 oz (1 lb)	450 g
1 ½ lb	750 g
2 lb	900 g
2 ¼ lb	1 kg
3 lb	1.4 kg
4 lb	1.8 kg

AMERICAN	METRIC	IMPERIAL
¼ tsp	1.2 ml	
½ tsp	2.5 ml	
1 tsp	5.0 ml	
½ Tbsp (1.5 tsp)	7.5 ml	
1 Tbsp (3 tsp)	15 ml	
¼ cup (4 Tbsp)	60 ml	2 fl oz
⅓ cup (5 Tbsp)	75 ml	2.5 fl oz
½ cup (8 Tbsp)	125 ml	4 fl oz
⅔ cup (10 Tbsp)	150 ml	5 fl oz
¾ cup (12 Tbsp)	175 ml	6 fl oz
1 cup (16 Tbsp)	250 ml	8 fl oz
1¼ cups	300 ml	10 fl oz (½ pint)
1½ cups	350 ml	12 fl oz
2 cups (1 pint)	500 ml	16 fl oz
2½ cups	625 ml	20 fl oz (1 pint)
1 quart	1 liter	32 fl oz

OVEN MARK	F	C	GAS
Very cool	250–275	130–140	½–1
Cool	300	150	2
Warm	325	170	3
Moderate	350	180	4
Moderately hot	375	190	5
	400	200	6
Hot	425	220	7
	450	230	8
Very hot	475	250	9

INDEX

(PAGE REFERENCES IN *ITALIC* REFER TO ILLUSTRATIONS)

Agave nectar, 21, 36, 37
Aguachiles, scallop, in volcano sauce, *78*, 79
Aguas frescas, 28, *38*, 39
Antojitos, 60–85
  ceviche *macho* (raw beef ceviche with jicama, lime, and habanero), 84
  guacamole con frutas (guacamole with fruit), 77
  güero chiles, pan-roasted, with blackened onions, *72*, 73
  hot dog, Mexican, with chipotle ketchup, 80
  lobster, chayote, and mango tostadas with chipotle crema, 69
  octopus salpicón with peppers, capers, and lemon, 74, *75*
  panuchos (corn empanadas with cheese and zucchini flowers), 66–68, *67*
  papas *locas* (roasted stuffed potatoes), 70
  salmon ceviche with ginger, apple, and cucumber, 82–83
  scallop aguachiles in volcano sauce, *78*, 79
  toritos (little peppers stuffed with garlic, shrimp, and Oaxaca cheese), 62–65, *63*
Avocado:
  cilantro sauce, 130
  guacamole con frutas (guacamole with fruit), 77
  tomatillo salsa (salsa verde), 135

Bar equipment, 44
BBQ sauce, piloncillo, 95
Beef:
  carne asado taco *vampiro*, *106*, 107–8
  chicken-fried steak taco with chile lime sauce, 109
  Coca-Cola shredded, taco, 104–5
  raw, ceviche with jicama, lime, and habanero, 84
  tongue, in lengua tacos with tomatillo salsa, 113
Beer:
  limonada, 33
  michelada, 49
  vaso *loco* (wild thing), 50
  Black beans with epazote, 140
  Blackberry mint margarita, 41
  Bloody Maria, 53
  BLT chicken taco, 117

Café de olla, 58
Carne asado taco *vampiro*, *106*, 107–8
Carnitas roasted with orange, milk, and pepper, tacos of, 110–12, *111*

Ceviche:
  macho (raw beef ceviche with jicama, lime, and habanero), 84
  salmon, with ginger, apple, and cucumber, 82–83
Chicken:
  BLT taco, 117
  fajita taco *dorado*, 114–16, *115*
  lemon-garlic, taco with mezcal, 119
  Chicken-fried steak taco with chile lime sauce, 109
  Chile(s), 105, 142–43
  de arbol, salsa de (hot sauce), 131
  dried, salsa with tequila (salsa borracha), 132
  güero, pan-roasted, with blackened onions, *72*, 73
  habanero mango salsa, 136
  lime sauce, 139
  rajas, mushroom, and corn taco with queso fresco, 122–24, *123*
  relleno taco with salsa *quemada*, 125
  serrano pineapple margarita, 36
  tequila *diablito* (devil's tequila), 26–27
Chipotle salsa, 138
Chocolate, hot, with agave and almonds, 59
Chupacabra:
  jugo de, 55
  mordida del (bite of the chupacabra), 54
Cilantro avocado sauce, 130
Clams, in vaso *loco* (wild thing), 50
Coca-Cola shredded beef taco, 104–5
Coffee:
  café de olla, 58
  iced Mexican, 56, *57*
Coleslaw, spicy, 103
Comal, 139
Corn:
  empanadas with cheese and zucchini flowers (panuchos), 66–68, *67*
  mushroom, and rajas taco with queso fresco, 122–24, *123*
  tostadas, 85
Crema, spicy, 121
Cucumber pineapple salsa, 137

Drinks, 18–59. *See also* Margaritas
  aguas frescas, 28, *38*, 39
  bar equipment, 44
  basics, 21
  bloody Maria, 53
  café de olla, 58

flavoring syrups, agave, or honey for, 36, 37
garnishes for, 22
hibiscus syrup for, 44
hot chocolate with agave and almonds, 59
iced Mexican coffee, 56, 57
jugo de chupacabra, 55
limonada, 33
michelada, 49
mojito, Mexican, 28, *29*
mordida del chupacabra (bite of chupacabra), 54
rico suave, 48
rimming glasses for, 23
sangria, 51
sangrita, 24
spicy verde (green Maria), 40
tequila *diablito* (devil's tequila), 26–27
vampira, 52
vaso *loco* (wild thing), 50
water and ice for, 28
Duck, chipotle, taco with duck chicharrón, pineapple cucumber salsa, and spicy crema, 120–21

Empanadas, corn, with cheese and zucchini flowers (panuchos), 66–68, *67*

Fish, 99
deep-fried, taco *capeado* with spicy coleslaw, 102–3
grilled, taco *zarandeado*, 96–99, *97*
salmon ceviche with ginger, apple, and cucumber, 82–83
smoked, taco, governor's (taco gobernador, Tijuana style), 100
tacos, mayonesa sauce for, 130

Ginger tangerine margarita, 34
Green Maria (spicy verde), 40
Guacamole con frutas (guacamole with fruit), 77
Güero chiles, pan-roasted, with blackened onions, *72, 73*

Habanero mango salsa, 136
Hibiscus:
margarita, 42, *43*
syrup, 44
Hot chocolate with agave and almonds, 59
Hot dog, Mexican, with chipotle ketchup, 80
Hot sauce (salsa de chiles de arbol), 131

Iced Mexican coffee, 56, *57*

Lamb, grilled, taco with salsa borracha and salsa verde, 93
Lengua tacos with tomatillo salsa, 113

Lettuce, in taco de lechuga with piloncillo BBQ shrimp, 94
Lime chile sauce, 139
Limonada, 33
Lobster, chayote, and mango tostadas with chipotle crema, 69

Mango(es):
habanero salsa, 136
tequila *diablito* (devil's tequila), 26–27
Margaritas:
blackberry mint, 41
fresh sweet and sour mix for, 31
hibiscus, 42, *43*
modern, 32
la paloma, 47
pineapple serrano, 36
sexy (margarito *amor*), 45
sol, 30
tangerine ginger, 34
watermelon, with candied cactus, 46
Marinade, carne asada, 108
Masa, spicy, 71
Mayonesa sauce for fish tacos, 130
Menus, 15–17
Mezcal, 20–21
infused, 26–27
Michelada, 49
Mint blackberry margarita, 41
Mojito, Mexican, 28, *29*
Mordida del chupacabra (bite of the chupacabra), 54
Mushroom, rajas, and corn taco with queso fresco, 122–24, *123*

Octopus salpicón with peppers, capers, and lemon, 74, *75*
Orange and orange-flavored liqueur:
margarita sol, 30
modern margarita, 32
rico suave, 48

Panuchos (corn empanadas with cheese and zucchini flowers), 66–68, *67*
Papas *locas* (roasted stuffed potatoes), 70
Peppers. *See also* Chile(s)
little, stuffed with garlic, shrimp, and Oaxaca cheese (toritos), 62–65, *63*
Perfecta, 49
Pico de gallo (fresh tomato salsa), 128
Piloncillo BBQ sauce, 95
Pineapple:
cucumber salsa, 137
serrano margarita, 36
Pork carnitas roasted with orange, milk, and pep-

pei, tacos of, 110–12, *111*
Potatoes, roasted stuffed (papas *locas*), 70

Rajas, mushroom, and corn taco with queso fresco, 122–24, *123*
Rico suave, 48
Rimming cocktail glasses, 23

Salmon ceviche with ginger, apple, and cucumber, 82–83
Salpicón, octopus, with peppers, capers, and lemon, 74, *75*
Salsas, 88, 126–38
    borracha (dried chile salsa with tequila), 132
    de chiles de arbol (hot sauce), 131
    chipotle, 138
    gobernador, 101
    mango habanero, 136
    pico de gallo (fresh tomato salsa), 128
    pineapple cucumber, 137
    quemada (roasted tomato salsa), 129
    tomatillo, raw, 133
    tomatillo, roasted, 134
    verde (avocado tomatillo salsa), 135
Sangria, 51
Sangrita, 24
Sauces:
    avocado cilantro, 130
    chile lime, 139
    hot (salsa de chiles de arbol), 131
    mayonesa, for fish tacos, 130
    piloncillo BBQ, 95
Scallop(s):
    aguachiles in volcano sauce, *78*, 79
    vaso *loco* (wild thing), 50
Seafood. *See also* Fish; Shrimp
    lobster, chayote, and mango tostadas with chipotle crema, 69
    octopus salpicón with peppers, capers, and lemon, 74, *75*
    scallop aguachiles in volcano sauce, *78*, 79
    vaso *loco* (wild thing), 50
Serrano pineapple margarita, 36
Shrimp:
    garlic, taco with poblano chile rajas, 92
    michelada with (*perfecta*), 49
    piloncillo BBQ, taco de lechuga with, 94
    taco *dorado*, 90, *91*
    vaso *loco* (wild thing), 50
Spicy verde (green Maria), 40
Sweet and sour mix, fresh, 31
Syrups, 28
    flavored or infused, 36, 37
    hibiscus, 44

simple, 36, 37

Tacos, 14, 86 125. *See also* Beef; Chicken; Fish; Shrimp
    basics, 88–89
    of carnitas roasted with orange, milk, and pepper, 110–12, *111*
    chile relleno, with salsa *quemada*, 125
    chipotle duck, with duck chicharrón, pineapple cucumber salsa, and spicy crema, 120–21
    grilled lamb, with salsa borracha and salsa verde, 93
    mushroom, rajas, and corn, with queso fresco, 122–24, *123*
Tangerine ginger margarita, 34
Tequila, 19–20, 24, 27. *See also* Margaritas
    bloody Maria, 53
    diablito (devil's tequila), 26–27
    dried chile salsa with (salsa borracha), 132
    infused, 26–27
    limonada, 33
    Mexican mojito, 28, *29*
    mordida del chupacabra, 54
    rico suave, 48
    and sangrita, 24
    spicy verde (green Maria), 40
    vampira, 52
    vaso *loco* (wild thing), 50
Tomatillo:
    avocado salsa (salsa verde), 135
    raw, salsa, 133
    roasted, salsa, 134
Tomato:
    fresh, salsa (pico de gallo), 128
    roasted, salsa (salsa *quemada*), 129
    sangrita, 24
Toritos (little peppers stuffed with garlic, shrimp, and Oaxaca cheese), 62–65, *63*
Tortillas, warming, 88
Tostadas, 85
    lobster, chayote, and mango, with chipotle crema, 69

Vampira, 52
Vaso *loco* (wild thing), 50
Vegetarian tacos, 122–25

Watermelon:
    agua fresca, 39
    margarita with candied cactus, 46
Wine, in sangria, 51

Zucchini flowers, corn empanadas with cheese and, 66–68, *67*